"Dating can be daunting for all pe[...] shy. Fortunately, Bonnie Jacobson offe[...] [...], most important, realistic dating advice for shy singles of all ages. Like the *Wizard of OZ*, she will help shy singles use their brain, develop their courage, and fill their heart as they follow the yellow-brick road to achieving dating success."

> —Bernardo J. Carducci, Ph.D., director of the Shyness Research Institute, professor of psychology at Indiana University Southeast, and author of *The Shyness Breakthrough*

"Dr. Jacobson takes up a widespread problem among those who want relationships but do not have them: debilitating shyness. Her approach is eminently practical and potentially beneficial for all who struggle with shyness. Written in a clear and breezy style, it's accessible to everyone."

> —Harold S. Bernard, Ph.D., president of the American Group Psychotherapy Association and clinical associate professor of psychiatry at New York University School of Medicine

"Bonnie Jacobson's compassion, wisdom, and boldness connects to the shy reader. Singles—and even others—will gather courage to make new attachments."

> —Myrna Weissman, Ph.D., professor of epidemiology in psychiatry and chief of the Division of Clinical and Genetic Epidemiology at Columbia University

"A powerful and gifted therapist, Bonnie Jacobson offers a brilliant road map towards courage and authentic self-confidence. *The Shy Single* is required reading for anybody navigating the difficult terrain of meeting and dating in these challenging times.

> —Linda Carter, Ph.D., director of the Family Studies Program at New York University Child Study Center

"Dr. Jacobson offers the shy single a sensitive, thoughtful, and practical approach to breaking out of the shell of shyness. Anyone who applies the insights in this useful book will finally be able to spread their wings and take flight in their own life."

> —Bonnie Maslin, Ph.D., psychologist and author of *Picking Your Battles: Winning Strategies for Raising Well-Behaved Kids*

THE SHY SINGLE

THE SHY SINGLE

A BOLD GUIDE

TO DATING

FOR THE

LESS-THAN-BOLD

DATER

BONNIE JACOBSON, PH.D.,
WITH SANDRA J. GORDON

RODALE

© 2004 by Bonnie Jacobson, Ph.D., and Sandra J. Gordon

Printed in the United States of America
Rodale Inc. makes every effort to use acid-free ∞, recycled paper ♲.

Book design by Drew Frantzen

Library of Congress Cataloging-in-Publication Data

Jacobson, Bonnie, Dr.
   The shy single : a bold guide to dating for the less-than-bold dater /
Bonnie Jacobson with Sandra J. Gordon.
      p.   cm.
   ISBN 1-57954-869-5 paperback
   1. Dating (Social customs)   2. Bashfulness.   I. Gordon, Sandra J.
II. Title.
HQ801.J233   2004
646.7'7—dc22   2003025407

Distributed to the book trade by St. Martin's Press
2 4 6 8 10 9 7 5 3 1 paperback

To my grandfather Joseph Andress, who was painfully shy, and Dr. Linda Carter, the inspiration for this book.

—B. J.

To Ron and Kym

—S. J. G.

ACKNOWLEDGMENTS

My gratitude is due to some of the people who helped transform the data from the therapy room to the publishing house. First is Meg Schneider. She believed in this work from day one and tirelessly attended the initial series of shyness workshops. She dedicatedly helped me codify the information that was unfolding. We were also assisted at that time by data collectors in each workshop: Dr. Victoria Stopak, Joan Rosillo, and Sloan Miller. I would love to mention some of the names of the workshop participants; their brilliant descriptions of the shy experience constitute the body of this book. But when they read it, they will know what ideas came directly from their own creative concepts. Dr. Stephanie Lyn and I turned the information that was collected into a Shyness Test, which has been statistically ratified as *the* measure of shyness calculation.

By this time, Meg assisted me in finishing our first complete manuscript. The initial edition was then transformed by several agents and writers along the way until it finally landed on the desk of my knowledgeable and supportive agent, Ms. Stacey Glick. She introduced me to Sandra Gordon, writer and collaborator from heaven. We were a cadre of no-nonsense professionals. Our threesome was then fortunate enough to encounter Jennifer Kushnier, editor at Rodale Press. A wonderful synergy ensued. We sped through the manuscript and had a finished product within a couple of months. Then Marcelle D'Argy Smith polished this text with love and ferocity. I am forever grateful and in awe of the professionalism of the entire team.

Not the least, I want to acknowledge my husband, Arie Shapira, who is constantly enthusiastic about and helpful with every project I undertake. As always, he completely shared this shyness adventure with me from its inception.

PREFACE

If there's a shy, single person I've met through my practice who truly wanted to be in a relationship, I've always been able to help them.

Well, that is a little bit of an exaggeration, but only insofar as some of my shy singles are not ready for marriage. Those individuals are working on unfinished business from their childhood families. But I am very optimistic that once they are comfortable with who they have become they will marry or find a significant love relationship if they so choose.

I have a friend named Elaine Housman who has an uncanny knack for connecting people who eventually marry. In fact, she was the matchmaker in my own marriage. The day I wrote this preface, there was a charming story in the *New York Times* about a man from Denver who advertised everywhere for a mate. He was a basketball player, and during an international competition, he held up a sign that he was looking for a wife. He is actually a shy person, but he used this strategy because he was determined. Elaine read about his plight and e-mailed him about her niece in Berkeley who is also a tall person. Today's *Times* article featured their wedding. It was a delightful story.

I began to reflect on Elaine's dedication and her skill. I then realized that I too have been devoting my life to relationships. They make me happy. When I participate in helping someone to end her loneliness and begin the next life challenge—a successful love relationship—it gives me tremendous joy. It feels as if I am part of a greater good that may help our beleaguered world.

It is much easier to pay attention to a squeaky wheel, someone who makes his request readily known. But shy people also need friends. Some shy people are a challenge even to themselves. To me, they have a treasure inside themselves waiting to be discovered. Because many of them are so appreciative, sensitive, quiet, and nondemanding, they usually play by the rules and do their best to fit in, rather than voice their requirements.

It's when I am conducting group therapy sessions that I experience my main "complaint" about shy people: They often do not equally participate in speaking, which, of course, is why they are in group in the first place. But even if all they ask of the group members is to pay attention to them, I believe that providing space so that another person can express him- or herself is a good skill for all of us to learn.

I began to develop an intense interest in shyness because of Melody, an intelligent, married engineer who was my client for many years. She was in a group for a long time and accomplished her original goals of healing her depression and developing a relationship with her parents, siblings, and extended family members where they came to respect her. Her husband was a lawyer and worked very long hours, some of them entertaining clients and socializing with his boss, who liked topless bars. At home, they rarely spoke or had sex.

Eventually Melody was ready to leave therapy, although her sex life was extremely limited. One day she tossed off a revelation about herself that I found startling. She said, "You probably don't realize this—I know it doesn't show—but I am a very shy person." Since she is a very articulate person, I had completely missed this. Melody said her shyness was almost paralyzing in two main areas: in bed with her husband and at large cocktail parties where she knew almost no one, such as those at a work convention. Her distress, and the realization that few professionals took the painful effects of shyness seriously, made me determined to explore all I could about it in adulthood.

We began running time-limited shyness workshops at the New York Institute for Psychological Change and developed an entire body of clinical data around the information we learned in these sessions. My practice is a combination of long-term group therapy and training workshops where other professionals learn how to conduct short-term shyness groups and workshops.

In the meantime, I also came to appreciate what some of my friends and family members were experiencing. I understood that what may have seemed to me like neglect, snobbery, disinterest, or laziness was shyness. Having a more compassionate explanation for some of the quietness of important friends and relatives at significant life crossroads allowed me to love them even when I felt abandoned or overlooked by them during times of need. I came to understand that we all show up in our own ways—not in the way that others may expect, but in the way that each of us is capable of giving.

So, I'd like to thank all my intelligent, sincere clients who have so enriched my life. I hope that our time together has been as enlightening for them as it has been for me.

And what happened to Melody and her husband? A recent e-mail informed me that they are living in England, they have a son, and she actually enjoys going to parties. There was a post-script: "By the way, Dr. J, I'm just loving my sex life."

CONTENTS

THE SHY SINGLE

"Life shrinks or expands in proportion to one's courage."
—*Anaïs Nin*

{ONE}

WHY CAN'T I JUST GET OVER MY SHYNESS?

CAROLINE, AN ATTRACTIVE, THIRTY-EIGHT-YEAR-OLD insurance executive, runs a business meeting with ease. She gives speeches to rooms full of scrutinizing strangers. She survives in a tough New York City job, after growing up in an Ohio farming community. But in social, meet-people situations, Caroline becomes dumbstruck with self-consciousness and negative thinking. She can't marshal the courage to meet someone—not online, not in a bar, not at work, not at an intimate dinner party. "I often think: 'Did I wear the right thing? I wish I could think of something compelling to say. Everyone here is more together than I am,'" she reported. Sadly, because Caroline typically measured what few words she could muster while hiding behind somber attire, she appeared aloof and uninteresting. In truth, when it came to dating she was simply shy, and shyness prevented her from getting what she wanted to complete her life: an honest and fulfilling relationship.

If this scenario sounds even remotely familiar, perhaps you can take comfort in these words: You are not alone. Shyness is common. According to the Shyness Institute, a nonprofit organization in Palo Alto, California, dedicated to adult shyness research, nearly 50 percent of the U.S. population—that's more than 140 million people—label themselves as chronically shy, to the degree that it presents a problem in some aspect of their lives. Extrapolate that to the worldwide population and you can imagine how many other Shys there are keeping you company.

Shyness tends to be selective. Like Caroline, there are probably a lot of things you can do in which your shyness isn't an issue—from charming a roomful of prospects into buying whatever you're selling to giving a party for friends whom you know well. But when you're on a date or milling about a dinner party of strangers, wham! Shyness can hit you like a blast of cold air. When you least expect it—when you *should* be having a good time—you're struck with a paralyzing fear that freezes your self-confidence.

IS SHYNESS HOLDING YOU BACK?

In my experience as a New York City psychologist, dating is the common denominator that triggers shyness among single men and women of all ages. In their quest to find someone with whom to share their lives, many of my clients tell me they're often plagued with such intense feelings of fear, rejection, and unworthiness that they grasp at any excuse to stay home. "But after a while, 'I'm under the weather' or 'I'm tired from a long week at work' doesn't cut it anymore," said Robert, a thirty-two-year-old chemist. "Your friends give up on you, and you realize that you're only hurting yourself by not forcing yourself to go out." But even if you do go out, you can find yourself haunted by feelings of numbing self-consciousness throughout the experience. Start a conversation or catch someone's eye? If only.

Pioneering shyness researchers such as Philip Zimbardo, Ph.D., at the Shyness Institute, and Bernardo J. Carducci, Ph.D., director of the Shyness Research Institute at Indiana University Southeast, find that shy people report they don't take advantage of social situations. They date infrequently, are less expressive verbally and nonverbally, and show less interest in others than do their nonshy counterparts. Indeed, although you can convince yourself otherwise (there is a lovely defense mechanism called denial), shyness can keep you from attending parties, participating in online and other dating services, and agreeing to go on the occasional set-up (blind date). It can limit your access to friends and potential life partners. Even if you do manage to go out, "it can end up feeling like a torturous waste of time," according to Caroline.

But here's the good news: So-called shrinking violets—or rather, people for whom dating-related shyness is an unmanaged obstacle—can wrestle their shyness to the ground and thrive. The information in this book can help you summon the courage you need to put yourself out there and meet that potentially special someone.

A Noticeable Trend

I know it's possible because the overwhelming majority of my clients are now success stories. In 1980, I founded the New York Institute for Psychological Change and established a program that offers treatments for a full spectrum of life problems. About a decade ago, I began to notice that client after client reported feeling socially incompetent, invisible to others, and fearful—especially on dates and in social situations. "I often feel like what I'm saying is wrong," said Jason, a twenty-something industrial engineer. Others frequently echoed this sentiment and further revealed that they micromanaged their own conversations when they were out socially, secretly labeling their input as unacceptable during the course of what should have been an enjoyable experience. Upon closer examination, as we dissected the dates and parties they attended, we found nothing askance had actually happened. I sensed that their feelings were part of an underlying concern.

Was it possible that these clients could be shy? Indeed. I began to realize that the word "shy" was frequently coming up either in their language or my thoughts—strikingly so. I then began to review articles in psychological journals, explore current research, consult with other colleagues regarding what exactly constitutes "shyness," and conduct time-limited shyness "workshops." Because of these workshops and psychotherapy groups, which are attended by hundreds of shy singles each year, I've gained an enlightened understanding of the ways in which singles experience this personality trait and render it manageable. The plight of the shy single has become my passion, especially today. With our futures so uncertain, the desire to connect with others in meaningful ways has become a collective priority. Singles who previously felt they had more time now feel a desire to get on with the show they call their lives.

It's Tough Out There

Despite the vast quantity of people who report feeling shy, there's little comfort in numbers because the dating climate has never been more intense, and it's everyone for himself (or herself). Popular television programs such as *Sex and the City*, *The Bachelor*, *The Bachelorette* (and other "reality"-based shows like them) encourage singles of all ages to assume a take-charge approach toward dating. Indeed, singles feel pressured to take charge. And Internet, e-mail, cell phones, and phenomena like ten-minute serial dating—are changing the conditions of the culture in which we live: depersonalizing it, accelerating it, and intensifying its complexity.

In this frenzied climate, patience is scarce for those who, like the shy, need time to warm up. There is a cultural tendency to quickly write off people without strong personalities—the proverbial squeaky wheels who get the grease. And, in the rush to be productive and not waste time, there are fewer opportunities than ever before to connect with one another. People commute wearing headphones while working on their laptops. They go from their apartments to the subway to the office, maintaining relationships with only a small circle of friends, colleagues, and family. Working longer hours, we have less time and energy to attend social functions. All told, there are few chances to get out there if you're single, and if you're shy, even fewer chances to hone your social skills, observe the interactions of others, and improve your social behavior (yes, you do get better with practice). "It's a jungle out there," said Megan, a twenty-seven-year-old interior designer, who was contemplating relocating to her former college town in Indiana. She suspected that meeting men would probably be easier there than in the urban jungle of New York City. "I'm not sure I have what it takes to survive here," she said. But moving was a gamble.

No matter where you go, your dating-related shyness is apt to follow. The solution is to strive to understand your shyness and focus on exactly how it impacts your life. Only then can you improve your dating skills and learn to manage your shyness so that it's not an impediment. You can even come to appreciate your shyness as you would any other of your unique characteristics, such as the color of your eyes, the wave of your hair, or the shape of your nose. In fact, I would argue that . . .

Being Shy Can Be a Good Thing

Although it can seem like shyness is holding you back socially, it's not a complete minus. Granted, there are times—such as at parties, where witty repartee and boisterous conversation are considered festive and desirable—when Shys blend into the woodwork. Maybe someone notices them, maybe not. But no one truly enjoys "party talk" all the time, because it's more of a performance than a representation of our true selves. We all want to feel close to others in meaningful and substantive ways. Achieving intimate contact with backslapping, fun-loving, laugh-a-minute acquaintances can be difficult for anyone.

Enter the person others count on for thoughtful, serious, or quietly humorous conversation, who naturally helps others feel their opinions count (that would be you). In general, the shy are good listeners. They tend to be naturally empathetic; they often remember details and ask thoughtful questions, and they usually are patient with the imperfections of others, since they consider themselves to be far from perfect. They're also not confrontational, generally giving people room to speak their minds without interrupting and inserting their own feelings into the picture or explaining why another person may be wrong. Shys spare people's feelings and refrain from declaring that someone's opinion is incorrect simply because they see things differently. Others are grateful to have Shys as sounding boards. These valuable traits leave others feeling acknowledged and respected. Sounds refreshing, doesn't it?

The shy also tend to convey an aura of mystery, strength, and intelligence. In this in-your-face world, there you are, in your quiet sort of way, leaving much to others' imaginations, keeping them guessing what's going on in your mind. When Shys, who tend not to seek center stage, do speak, people are often eager to listen and trust their opinions. Like beautifully presented haute cuisine at an expensive restaurant, the psychology of minimalism applies. Less can be much more.

If you're shy, there's another bonus: You probably notice many things because the shy tend to be observers. In your mezzanine seat in life, you're able to sit back and see the bigger picture. You take in details others often miss. For some, like Sam, a single man who writes for a newspaper, shyness is an occupational asset. "If I weren't shy," Sam said one day, "I wouldn't be so sensitive or observant, which are two qualities I need in my writing."

Moreover, others naturally trust you. Your quietness leads people to believe their secrets are safe with you. While this doesn't necessarily follow—the shy can be as tempted as anyone else to reveal a juicy story—you can enjoy the sense that others regard you as someone who keeps their own counsel.

You probably also think things through. Many assertive personalities act first and reflect later. They're not afraid to react, and so they do. Maybe you know someone who is aggressive, wonderfully funny and clever, but who simply has no idea when she's hurting other people's feelings or exhausting them with self-centeredness. The shy, on the other hand, tend to plan first and act later. Forethought can help you weigh your options and move forward, prepared for various outcomes. It also spares those around you from being hurt by your impulsive remarks or ill-advised behaviors. Most important, your attention to matters before they happen leaves you well prepared. If you're blessed with heightened sensitivity, like many shy people are, you're rarely caught off guard.

THE SCIENCE OF SHYNESS

Despite myriad assets, shyness conjures up a number of images to which many adults would rather not lay claim: toddlers hiding behind their mothers' skirts, children standing alone on the playground, teens unable to speak at the prom, and even trembling kittens. Few people think of a highly successful scientist, a Park Avenue socialite fund-raiser, a well-established therapist, or a powerful businessman as shy. But they can be. Shyness knows no boundaries. It can affect people of all social strata. Education, economics, success, and age don't faze it because shyness is, at least in part, genetic, like eye color or height.

More specifically, shyness is an inborn trait, a physical dimension of your personality called temperament. Shyness can more fully express its biological mandate if it's also triggered by life factors, such as your infant environment, your childhood experiences, or your relationship with your parents. Since shyness is partially governed by genes, it is only beginning to be understood by scientists. One study conducted by Daniel R. Weinberger, M.D., at the National Institute of Mental Health in Washington, D.C., suggests that inheriting a shorter version of a single gene—the human serotonin transporter gene, SLC6A4—appears to predispose people to fearfulness, which is the basis of shyness. The study, which involved functional Magnetic Resonance Imaging scans of the brain, looked at how people with different variations of this gene responded to pictures of individuals who appeared frightened. According to the researchers, humans sense danger by taking cues from others, which is why merely looking at pictures of people who look fearful can cause fear.

In Weinberger's study, when subjects were shown photos of scared faces, those who inherited one or two variants of a shorter SLC6A4 gene displayed more activity in the amygdala, the "hub of fear" structure in the brain. The study suggests that those with a shorter SLC6A4 gene might experience slightly higher levels of anxiety as a response to fear or perhaps be inherently more vigilant.

Compared to adults, shy children have received much more attention from the scientific community. For several decades, Jerome Kagan, Ph.D., author of *Galen's Prophecy: Temperament in Human Nature*, and his colleagues at Harvard University have been studying the concept of inborn shyness. Kagan's work reveals that children differ in their initial tendencies to approach unfamiliar people, objects, and circumstances. His work also demonstrates that physiological differences—such as faster heart rates and jerky movements of the arms and legs in response to stimuli, like mobiles in motion and tape recordings of human voices—appear in shy babies as young as two months of age. Children born with a tendency toward shyness (from 15 to 20 percent of all newborns) belong to the temperamental category called "inhibited." On the other hand, "uninhibited" children (also 15 to 20 percent of newborns) demonstrate curiosity and sociability towards the unfamiliar. (The rest fall somewhere in between the two extremes of timidity and boldness.)

Kagan's research also indicates that environment plays a role in determining whether inborn traits of inhibition will remain dominant as children mature. Uninhibited kids with overprotective parents, for example, can become more fearful if they're constantly being told to "watch out." Likewise, an environment that supports and gently encourages the needs of inhibited children may result in them moving through life manifesting quiet, sensitive, or more thoughtful behaviors in most situations, rather than overt fear.

Upon reaching adulthood, if a person has an activated shyness gene, his shyness may surface sporadically. With my shy clients, I have found that their inborn temperament is expressed differently in various life roles. In situations in which they feel comfortable and know *how to be*—like Caroline's having no trouble

SHYNESS VS. SOCIAL ANXIETY DISORDER

Frequently I encounter clients who are merely shy—they show symptoms of fearfulness, blushing, inhibited speech, and extreme self-consciousness in social situations—but who have been diagnosed by a previous therapist as having social anxiety disorder (aka social phobia). In some cases, shy people do develop social phobia. (When shyness isn't diagnosed or understood as a critical part of your suffering, its symptoms can persist and worsen.) But many don't. What's the difference? If you're shy, being spontaneous is tough; you feel unsure and extremely self-conscious. In those moments, you fear being judged as "less than" by others (but, really, you're projecting onto others your own self-critical thoughts).

Nonetheless, you may weaken your ability to express yourself and develop what I call a low tolerance for being in the company of others whom you think are judging you. If this sensitivity becomes extreme, you may become socially phobic, which is a fear of going out in public. Someone who is simply shy, on the other hand, doesn't fear the social world, per se. In fact, many of my clients (especially those who are shy around people they know) enjoy going out and meeting people. But they find it difficult to present their true selves in close relationships, or they become stricken with self-consciousness and inhibition when they're trying to impress someone they're interested in. They're afraid to be "known" because of fear of rejection and ultimate abandonment.

If you believe you suffer from social anxiety disorder, medication may help ease your symptoms so you can venture out on dates and other social situations. In the appendix (starting on page 215), I'll explore social anxiety disorder in more detail and discuss when I typically suggest that my clients see a psychopharmacologist for medication, as well as the medication currently recommended and available.

giving presentations to important clients—they might not be shy at all. But in other aspects of their lives, like dating or trying to get past the initial conversational awkwardness at a dinner party, they just flounder. They're not on terra firma. (Sound familiar?) And that's what makes dating-related shyness such a torturous enigma. Many of my clients report thinking: 'What's the matter with me? I did it at work, why can't I do it at a dinner party (or on a date, at a bar, or online)?' After all, because shyness is selective, you know what it feels like to *not* be shy, to feel empowered, to be confident, and to bask in the admiration, approval, or acceptance of others.

Typically, many of my clients downplay their affliction and chide themselves for being unable to "get over" their shyness. (After all, they reason, they are free from shyness at work and other non-dating situations.) They get angry with themselves for not being able to step out with confidence and flair and make the world notice. Their disappointment in themselves for failing only exacerbates their dating anxieties and triggers feelings of hopelessness, frustration, even depression. But shyness isn't a death sentence. Yes, it can be maddening, especially when you know yourself to not be shy in all situations. The best you can do is accept it, work with it, and live with it. Welcome it into your life like a puppy coming in from the rain. You might as well, because it's part of who you are, like your curly hair or your skinny arms. Yet shyness is a trait that can be managed, not unlike straightening your hair or working out at the gym.

WORK WITH WHAT YOU'VE GOT

At its core, dating-related shyness is a fear of the unfamiliar. You're unsure of what's expected or whether you can live up to what's required of you. For some Shys, the situations in which they feel unsure tend to center around strangers or acquaintances. For others, the roles in which they feel awkward tend to be in private arenas such as making love or being natural around someone they've dated for a while. (As the stakes increase and a relationship takes shape, they experience a kind of performance anxiety and fear they'll "blow it." More on this in chapter nine.)

Yet, no matter what kind of dating-related shyness you have, once you recognize that shyness is something you can't will away or fully outgrow, you can begin to understand and accept it, and start to work with it. And that's the general philosophy of this book: *Shyness is a trait you can manage.* It gave me great pleasure when Miles, a formerly shy single, said, "Once I realized that my dating shyness is a part of me, my shyness went to a different level. I'm still shy, but I definitely can handle it better. It's just another part of me, not who I am."

Miles had been working at redefining himself for the better part of a year, trying the various strategies I'll outline in this book, when he met his girlfriend, Nell, at a bar. What ultimately worked for him? "When I had a moment of dating anxiety, like when I was trying to participate in conversations in bars and other group settings, I let myself experience it and not run away," he said. "It passed in a few minutes." His hard-won courage paid off; Miles and Nell now enjoy their togetherness. But Miles knows he can call upon the shyness-management skills he learned if he should someday resume his single status.

LET ME BE YOUR DATING COACH

The chapters in *The Shy Single* represent a distilled version of my decade of practice conducting shyness workshops and group therapy for shy singles. It's my hope that this book will not only help you better understand yourself so you become less self-critical, but will also give you the tools you need to maneuver through dating situations with courage and confidence. No matter what your age or dating experience, you'll learn how to break out of the prison of shyness by managing your fear. As your dating coach, I'll help you define your dating style, determine your priorities, explore your current patterns, and set and accomplish your goals. More specifically, I'll help you learn how to more effectively:

- "Work a room" and get past the initial awkwardness of introductions at parties.

- Approach someone who looks interesting.

- Participate in engaging dinner conversation and bridge uncomfortable silences.

- Ask someone out.

- End a date gracefully.

- Handle sexual advances (making or receiving them).

- Navigate the world of online dating.

To the nonshy, these dating activities may sound like child's play. Make conversation at a dinner party? What's so difficult about that? But in fact, even Nonshys sometimes have trouble with these "skills." If you're shy, however, they're often major obstacles. With that in mind, this book will discuss shyness management for "classic" Shys—those who are shy around people they don't know well, as an estimated 75 percent of shy people are, according to surveys conducted by Carducci. In chapter nine, I'll also cover an often-overlooked category: those who are shy around people they know. They're the people who become shy in intimate situations.

No matter what type of shy single you are (some of us are both), this book will help you manage dating-related shyness by making small increments of change in each stage of a relationship—from meeting someone, making conversation, and getting to know him to becoming intimate, saying "I love you," and planning for the future—or not. (Yes, shyness can also prevent you from ending a relationship that's not working.) Keep in mind that this advice isn't designed to be one-size-fits-all. In fact, I encourage you to personalize it. Feel free to go on your own and *not* take my suggestions verbatim. And, of course, if something occurs to you that you'd like to try that's not in these pages, by all means, go for it! It just might work. If it doesn't, you'll no doubt learn something useful about yourself. With shyness management, like most things in life, what doesn't work out can often provide as much insight as what does.

THE SHYNESS ATTACK

It's important to note that the goal of *The Shy Single* is *not* to help you become unshy and, perhaps, violate your basic nature. Rather, the goal is to teach you how to function *despite* your pounding heart and sweaty palms and to develop satisfying relationships by working through the fear that may otherwise overwhelm you. Central to its theme are specific steps, which I'll discuss in chapters three, four, and five, that you can take to manage what I call a shyness attack. The shyness attack has three distinct stages:

1. **The fear of initiation.** During this first stage, shy singles feel overwhelmed and paralyzed by the fear of rejection and uncertainty. They simply can't make the first move—to say hello, make eye contact, ask someone out for a drink, or initiate intimacy. In the many groups of shy singles I've counseled, as soon as I raise the issue of taking that initial step in any of these situations, the floodgates open. In one of my workshops, Leslie, a forty-one-year-old sales representative, aptly described the fear of initiation: "At a recent party at a friend's apartment, I took off my coat and walked into the bedroom to pile it on a chair. Instead, I folded it neatly and then folded it again. I could hear the buzz from the living room of the other guests talking and having fun. But I wasn't sure I knew more than a few people in there. I caught myself picking someone's coat off the floor and draping it neatly on the bed, smoothing out a crease in the arm. I realized I'd actually rather deal with coats than go

into the other room. Good grief." That's a perfect example of the fear of initiation.

2. **Circuit overload.** This second stage of a shyness attack occurs when Shys venture out socially: They've entered the party; they're on a first, second, or third date; they meet an interesting-looking stranger. In this stage, after sitting on many thoughts and emotions, shy singles can feel overloaded, yet they know it's time to talk and connect. The result: When they're ready to speak, either they shut down and barely converse at all (freezing), or a torrent of words rushes out (flooding). Freezing is akin to being starstruck, but around regular folks, not celebrities. A classic example: The hostess introduces you to a good-looking man at a party, with an appropriate opening line, such as, "Meet Dennis. He just got back from Finland," and all you can offer is, "Oh," while another partygoer who overhears the introduction waltzes in with an engaging question, such as, "Was it for work or pleasure?" and they're off and chatting.

   Unlike freezers, flooders do the opposite: They babble. And while initially what they're saying can be lively and interesting, it becomes tiresome if they don't let others participate or show interest in their thoughts or ideas. In their quest to fill the conversational void, flooders fear they may also reveal over-the-top, inappropriate information, either personal or unrelated, thereby running the risk of sounding desperate or illogical—and ultimately alienate their listeners. "When my date asked me what my plans were for the summer, I blurted out, 'I really want a cat,'" said Shelly, a shy single in her early thirties who works in advertising. "He didn't know me well enough to care about my cat fetish and must've thought I was truly wacky."

   As the flooder speaks, she hears a constant internal litany of self-criticism, such as, "Why'd I say that? What am I rambling about? If I stop, he'll talk and then I won't know what to say. Oh, why can't I be like that amusing person across the room?" If that sounds familiar, there's hope. With practice, even shy singles prone to flooding can become engaging conversationalists who tell amusing or interesting anecdotes and leave room for others to tell theirs.

3. **Payback.** The final stage of a shyness attack is payback: the hours, days, or weeks after a social event or date when shyness sufferers obsess over everything they said or did—or didn't say or do. Hypercritical of their "performance," they punish themselves by reliving their blunders or omissions, which they're convinced have ruined any chance for future contact. Payback differs from learning by trial and error, in which self-reviewers lovingly critique their strengths and weaknesses in a social encounter to further empower themselves. With payback, a Shy obsessively criticizes himself for blunders—real or imagined. This kind of punishment unintentionally weakens the self and depletes self-esteem.

With the shyness attack at its core, *The Shy Single* will help you learn how to embrace the notion of shyness as a trait that you can handle skillfully and responsibly. Knowledge and acceptance are formidable weapons. You'll learn to recognize the triggers of a shyness attack and take steps to diminish the intensity of your fear. You'll build the self-confidence it takes to go out socially, venturing beyond your comfort zone again and again. (Although it only takes one Mr. or Ms. Right, successful dating is, after all, often a numbers game.)

You won't be on your own on this exciting and rewarding personal journey. Consider me your safety net as well as your cheerleader. As your dating coach, I'll be right there with you, dispensing my highly personalized advice to bolster your courage—every step along the way. So get ready for my guidelines and real-world insights from my clients that will show you how to achieve the social life you deserve.

"To have courage for whatever comes in life—
everything lies in that."

—Mother Teresa

{TWO}

WHAT'S YOUR DATING STYLE?

LIKE HAVING BLUE EYES OR CURLY HAIR, dating is very individual. Do you do better in bars? At parties? At work? One on one? Online? With people you know well? Or with those you've just met? Your answers to these and other questions are the basis of your dating style—the dating formats and venues that accentuate your personality and make you feel comfortable. When you become aware of your style by examining your dating history, you can use it to your advantage by choosing dating situations that highlight your strengths and increase your comfort level. That's important for everyone to do, but especially if you're shy. This chapter will help you identify your dating style so that you have a blueprint for dating. Then you can pinpoint the types of dating situations in which you've had success and build upon them. You'll be in control.

To determine their dating styles, one of the first things participants in my shyness workshops do is take a fifty-question quiz called "Your Dating Profile." Dr. Stephanie Lin and I developed this for an unpublished study in conjunction with New York

University as part of her doctoral thesis. The quiz provides an inventory of symptoms and experiences commonly felt by shy people. It offers you an opportunity to identify the types of dating experiences in which you most acutely feel shy. Your answers to the quiz will also give you an idea of how intensely shyness affects your social life. I encourage you to take the quiz now.

YOUR DATING PROFILE

As you consider each question below, check the box adjacent to the statements that apply to you, the ones in which "Yes, that's me" comes to mind.

In dating/social situations:

☐ 1. I'm extremely comfortable in some highly social situations. It just depends on where I am and who I'm with.

☐ 2. I'm sometimes unable to speak. I have thoughts to contribute but I tend to keep them to myself.

☐ 3. I'm capable of becoming so anxious that all my thoughts, except self-critical ones, disappear.

☐ 4. I often get angry with myself for lacking the courage to approach someone or contribute to a conversation.

☐ 5. I'm often jealous of others who speak freely, those who are the "life of the party."

☐ 6. After many encounters, I torture myself with self-critical thoughts.

☐ 7. I sometimes have trouble initiating a conversation.

☐ 8. I'm very sensitive as to whose turn it is to speak in a conversation, and I'm scared of saying too much. (Whose turn is it? She said this, so should I say that?)

☐   9. I feel rejected if someone I'm conversing with doesn't meet me halfway and respond as enthusiastically as I do.

☐   10. I'm lonely.

☐   11. I frequently bow out of or refuse invitations and choose solitude because going out is too stressful.

☐   12. I regularly feel "different" from others, except in specific, comfortable roles, like when I'm around my family or at work.

☐   13. I feel disconnected if I'm separated from someone I feel close to.

☐   14. I often feel overwhelmed or "invaded" by too much attention.

☐   15. I frequently feel invisible.

In general:

☐   16. I have friendships in a series as opposed to several at the same time.

☐   17. I like constancy rather than the unpredictable. I'm usually not comfortable taking advantage of unplanned opportunities or activities.

☐   18. I often procrastinate to avoid conflict.

☐   19. I often take a back seat to more powerful or outgoing people and let them lead a conversation.

☐   20. I usually fear that I've been offensive after criticizing another person.

☐   21. I resist making decisions except in very specific roles.

☐   22. I experience feelings intensely—someone else's and mine.

☐ 23. I rarely ask for what I want from others.

☐ 24. I'm frequently unsure whether I deserve what I want.

☐ 25. When I'm distressed, I often say nothing at the time, build up steam, and then explode later either outwardly or inwardly, directly or indirectly. (Indirect explosions can take the form of addictive behavior.)

☐ 26. I avoid initiating sex.

☐ 27. I feel overwhelmed if a partner initiates sex.

☐ 28. I sometimes seek anonymous sexual encounters.

☐ 29. I have difficulty negotiating for myself and am loathe to say what I want.

☐ 30. I have trouble "giving" to myself, like allowing myself a reward for a project well done at work.

☐ 31. I participate in some form of addictive behavior (drinking, eating, spending, etc.).

☐ 32. I frequently laugh whether something is funny or not.

☐ 33. I need to feel well prepared before doing almost anything.

☐ 34. I don't enjoy change.

☐ 35. I lie to avoid confrontations.

☐ 36. I want to do everything perfectly.

I think I'm often erroneously described or thought of as:

☐ 37. Withdrawn, when I really feel scared.

☐ 38. Detached, when I'm really afraid to reach out.

☐ 39. Self-important, when my silence is usually due to the opposite feeling.

☐ 40. Snobbish, when my aloofness is really a fear of taking that first step, like introducing myself at a party.

☐ 41. Drawing attention to myself because I'm quiet.

I'm sometimes described as:

☐ 42. A good listener.

☐ 43. Nonthreatening and kind.

☐ 44. Accepting of others.

☐ 45. Sincere.

☐ 46. Trustworthy.

In occasional dating/social situations, I have physical symptoms like:

☐ 47. Blushing.

☐ 48. Sweaty palms.

☐ 49. Stammering.

☐ 50. Self-conscious laughter.

Total number checked: _____

If your shyness is pervasive, you probably checked more than thirty-six questions. (If your checks number forty or more, you may be suffering from social phobia, which is more than shyness. Turn to the appendix, starting on page 215, for more information.) If your shyness is moderate and doesn't affect you in every dating or social encounter, you checked twenty-four to thirty-five questions. If your dating-related shyness is slight and only affects you occasionally, you answered yes to between twelve and twenty-three questions. Anything lower would indicate you have a shy moment or two but not a serious, painful shyness problem. Based on your answers, you might be someone who suffers from shyness less than you thought, or perhaps more pervasively (having passed your symptoms off as other problems, such as anxiety, nervousness, or work-related fatigue).

Your profile can both help you understand the extent to which shyness impacts your dating experiences and guide you in correctly assessing situations so that you'll be less likely to self-blame and -criticize. (An example of a healthy assessment: *I'm not boring. I'm just feeling shy, and I accept it.*) Your profile will also help you reduce the number and severity of dating-related shyness attacks, which I'll discuss in detail starting in chapter three.

YOUR DATING STYLE

If you're like many shy singles, you probably never realized that you're capable of having your own dating style. Perhaps you're accustomed to regarding yourself like goods in a buyer's market. "At a party recently, I was so mad at myself because I just sat there, waiting for the women to notice me," said Paul, a thirty-three-year-old marketing executive in one of my workshops. Many others in the group sympathized. It's a common lament that's often not verbalized, but it can radiate from your facial expression and body language: *Please initiate the social exchange. Please approach me. Someone do something.* As a shy single, perhaps you can't imagine that you could be the one to come up with a plan to include others (who would be thrilled if you did). But, in fact, you can become the initiator if you know your dating style and work with it to increase your comfort level. Here's how.

Step One: Draw from Past Experience

First recall previous dating experiences, as far back as junior high school if necessary, and ask yourself the questions on page 24. If, in your opinion, you haven't dated enough to draw from past experience, think about social events you've attended in which you felt particularly comfortable. Record your answers in the spaces provided.

- What's the best date (or interaction with someone I was interested in) I've *ever* had? Where was I? Who was I with? Why did it go so well?

_____

_____

_____

_____

_____

- What other dates (or social interactions) have come close to that all-time best date? Where was I? Who was I with? Why did they go so well?

_____

_____

_____

_____

_____

_____

_____

_____

- What's the best *recent* date (or interaction with someone I was interested in) I've had? Where was I? Who was I with? Why did it go so well?

_____

_____

_____

_____

_____

Can you spot any similarities or patterns in your answers? For instance, was the setting for these best dates a quiet one, like a trip to a museum? Did they result from a set-up or a mutual interest, like scuba diving? Were they last-minute, or planned weeks in advance?

In broad strokes, my pattern seems to be:

_____

_____

_____

_____

_____

_____

To identify dating situations you may want to avoid, record your answers to a counter set of questions below. Again, feel free to go back as far as junior high school.

- What's the worst date (or interaction with someone I was interested in) I've *ever* had? Where was I? Who was I with? Why did it go so badly?

_____

_____

_____

_____

_____

_____

- What other dates (or other social interactions) have come close to that all-time worst one? Where was I? Who was I with? Why did they go so badly?

_____

_____

_____

_____

_____

_____

_____

· What's the worst *recent* date (or interaction with someone I was interested in) I've had? Where was I? Who was I with? Why did it go so badly?

_____

_____

_____

_____

_____

Can you spot any similarities or patterns in your answers?

_____

_____

_____

_____

_____

Step Two: Analyze Your Current Dating Pattern

Review your appointment book from the past six months. What sort of social events did you actually put into your book? Which ones did you go to? More specifically, were you ever in situations that other single people attended? If so, you have valuable information about your present social life that can help you develop a successful dating strategy. Make a note of what happened at each event in the space below. Where were you? Who were you with?

_____

_____

_____

_____

_____

_____

_____

Step Three: Put It All Together

Now, look over your answers to the questions in steps one and two and see whether you can create a composite picture of your best venues, the types of people with whom you are comfortable, and what you need in order to feel at ease and connect with another person. In evaluating your answers, focus on whether your best and worst dating experiences were with people you knew or with strangers. Were they first-time dates? Third or fourth dates? Were they in a group? One on one? Were you in your neighborhood? On vacation? At work? At a party?

_____

_____

_____

_____

_____

In evaluating his answers, Alec, a shy loan officer in his mid-thirties, realized that he felt best when he was with women who weren't shy. "I can recall situations in which neither the woman I was with or myself barely said a word other than 'hello' at the beginning of the date and 'well, goodnight' at the end of it. We'd go to a movie with one or two other couples and watch it in excruciating detail. It's painful to think about," he said, cringing at his high school memories. Alec's pattern repeated throughout college. Still, those memories provide a solid base of information he can now use to his advantage. "I now understand that outgoing women are a better fit for me so I try to spot 'the talkers' at events early on and introduce myself," he said.

In evaluating her answers to these questions, Abby, a shy nurse in her late twenties, realized that she didn't do well in social settings in which she couldn't quietly talk, where she had to shout to be heard, like in a bar or at a concert. "I'm not an obvious beauty, someone who is going to turn heads," she said. "But I do have an intellectual side that gets going if I'm with the right person. I think I'm looking for someone who gets that part of me, someone I can match wits with," she said. At that moment, her eyes lit up. She realized that too much of her social life revolved around going to loud bars with her friends—in essence, hiding in plain sight. It likely wasn't a good fit for her dating style since the noise level in many bars can make talking difficult. "From now on, I'm going to focus on going to things that offer me the opportunity to chat, like cocktail parties, networking events, and lectures," Abby decided.

Although it helps to have a *general* idea of your best dating venues, you might be tempted to fine-tune them. If gyms have worked for you in the past, for example, you could ask yourself: *Was I in a class or working out on the machines or weight equipment?* If you've had success in bars, you might ask: *What kind of bar was I in? A sports bar? An upscale martini bar?* In fact, you can examine any successful dating experi-

COACH'S CORNER

The most rewarding interactions are the ones that bring out your best self. If you have wit, you'll want to use it. If you have dynamic ideas, you're going to want to express them. If you have deep sensitivities, you'll want to address them. But they all need a forum—a comfortable location and receptive people—which is what your dating style should reflect.

ence to tease out its workable components. But be careful not to let obsessive details become a dating obstacle. Otherwise, your dating style can begin to sound like the board game Clue: I do well in bars, by fireplaces, on weeknights, after one drink, wearing something blue. A dating style like that—far too limiting!—can thwart you from experiencing the wide variety of

LOCATION, LOCATION, LOCATION

Most single people I know often find themselves, without a plan, in one of two places where other singles congregate: a bar or the gym. As clichéd as these classic pick-up spots can seem, I wouldn't discount them as places to meet someone. Bars might not work for some people, but maybe they can for you. The same for your health club. It's worth asking yourself, *Have I ever met someone I could date at either of these places?* If so, did these people turn out to be the type of individuals you were specifically looking for? If they did, you may wish to incorporate more of these experiences into your dating repertoire.

Both locations have their plusses and minuses. One negative for bars is they have a reputation for being "meat markets"—that is, places where people go to "hook up" for the night, not to look for someone to date. Still, it's safe to say that some people who are interested in finding someone special frequent bars, because that's where potentially like-minded single people tend to congregate periodically. A downside of the gym scene is that it may be overly focused on physical appearance, rather than personality and character. This emphasis could be a problem for the shy, especially if you're somewhat embarrassed to show your body. On the other hand, the physical fitness climate of the gym could be an advantage to you, especially at first, because you're actively engaged. Similarly, bars with loud music playing offer a muffling cocoon. Both provide exposure and contact without pressuring you to converse. Bottom line: There are no hard-and-fast rules for dating because it's so individual. What doesn't work for another person may in fact be just the ticket for you.

possibilities or dating situations that could lead to discovering someone right for you.

Start Today

If you have no way to determine your current social pattern because you don't have anything written down on pages 24–27, you don't go out, or because you can't remember what you did last week, then begin today. For the next month, write down every social thing you do, from having a meal at the neighbors', to going to your cousin's wedding, to going ice-skating with your colleagues. After a few weeks, you'll begin to notice which events make you feel good and which ones feel obligatory, even painful.

The goal of this exercise is to establish a protocol that truly matches what you like to do and makes you comfortable. That's the solid foundation upon which you can build your dating life. Eventually, you'll be able to experiment with fresh adventures that might initially provoke anxiety—but only because they're new to you.

BEING SHY AND 'FESSING UP

Knowing your dating style—particularly whether you're shy around people you know or don't know—can also help your partners. Let's say, for example, you're shy around people you know, not with strangers. This means that during the course of dating, you're going to become increasingly self-conscious as you see more of any one person. After the first few dates, you're going to want to shut down because, in your mind, the stakes increase, not decrease. If you know this about yourself, it can actually help to tell the other person, "I'm shy, especially as I get to know someone." You may have to keep repeating, "No, it's true, I really am shy," because your dates may not believe you because of your initial outgoing style.

If you're *not* up-front about your latent shyness, the other person may feel rejected when you start to withdraw. "At that point, my dates usually get frustrated and start to pressure me to define the relationship," said Bryce, a commercial real estate broker in his late thirties. "Then I feel intimidated into having the 'where are we going

with this' conversation way before I'm ready." (More on that in chapter seven.)

Similarly, if you're shy from day one, but tend to become less so as time goes on, it helps to confess, "Look, I'm a little shy . . . " To muster up the courage, think of the golden rule: Do not do to another what you don't want done to you. In other words, if you were with someone who's shy, you'd be relieved if he confessed that he's shy, wouldn't you? Otherwise, you might rapidly begin to feel rejected (possibly your most prevalent social emotion). One of my shy clients, Alice, tells everyone she's shy from the first day. Initially, it was hard for her to do, but now she's gotten over that inhibition. "It's a miracle to me that I can tell people right up front that I'm shy, but it helps them understand what's going on—and feel less rejected by the fact that I don't talk a lot in the beginning," she said. "I've found that things just go much better."

DATING AGAINST THE TIDE

There will be times when you find yourself out of your element, in surroundings or the company of others with whom you think you're poorly matched. But don't leave as soon as possible or avoid these potentially uncomfortable situations altogether.

Instead, stay flexible. After all, even a vegetarian can find something to order at a steakhouse—and it could be delicious, and even better than you expected. You never know what might come of it. That go-with-the-flow strategy worked for Susan, a shy single in her thirties who works for a German bank. "I met the guy I'm now dating at a bar in the Hamptons," she told the group one evening. "Bars aren't my style because it's usually too hard for me to break into a conversation, especially if I'm standing in a group and everyone is trying to impress. But that one time, I agreed to go along, and I met someone truly special."

When you find yourself in dating situations that aren't your forte, like Susan did, just be aware of it and cut yourself some slack. You might say to yourself, *Oh, this isn't where I do my best, so whatever I do here is a freebie. Whatever happens, happens.* By doing so, you'll help take the pressure off yourself and perhaps even build on your positive dating history. All told, if the night or event happens to go well, an intimidating dating venue may seem less so. When I asked Susan if she had any strategies for getting through the bar experience that evening she met Matthew, she said, "I reminded myself that I usually don't do well in bars, but this time, if I meet someone, I'm going to make myself keep talking, no matter how self-conscious I feel. And that's what did it." Susan chose that night to stretch her skills because, well, she was at a bar and bars—top on her list of dating don'ts—didn't "count." Her practice paid off brilliantly. "Matthew and I are making plans for the future, and that's a big thing for me," she told the group.

DETERMINE YOUR DATING OBJECTIVES

Determining your dating objectives is as important a part of your overall dating plan as identifying your dating style. Knowing what you truly want out of socializing—that is, your dating destination—can help you set reachable long- and short-term goals and avoid wasting time. Without objectives, it's easy to flounder and backtrack into safe territory—like continuing to date someone you're not interested in just because he keeps asking you out. (More on that in chapter seven.)

Setting Long-Term Goals

Take a moment now to think about your long-term dating goals. What are they? Do you hope for marriage and possibly children someday? Do you want marriage but not children? For most shy singles, marriage—to the right person—may be an obvious answer. But for you, it may not be, especially if you've been married before. Take a moment now to write your goals in the space that follows.

My long-term goals for dating are:

Maybe your long-term goal is to be exposed to as many different types of people as possible. That was Gillian's goal when she came to my workshop. Freshly divorced, she wasn't ready to make commitments. But she was eager to meet as many different men as she could. "I never really got the chance to date because I got married in college," she explained. "I was shy and, well, he asked, so I said yes. But almost immediately after the ceremony, I started wondering what it would be like to be with other types of men. My husband was a blond-haired, blue-eyed, left-handed Lutheran like myself. People said we looked like twins. And it wasn't that I wasn't happy. I just sort of had the feeling that I hadn't done my homework."

Gillian's short-term goals centered around playing the field, but especially men who were culturally different from her. During the next six months, she scoured the local papers for social events to attend in her new ethnic neighborhood where she might possibly meet people who could expand her dating horizons. She went to several and planned to keep going. Based on the goals she set for herself, that was an excellent plan.

COACH'S CORNER

If your life goal does *not* include marriage, at least not now (and maybe never), then your dating objectives could be vastly different than if you're marriage-minded. You may just want to play the field, or find someone else who doesn't want to get married, or simply have something to do every Saturday night. Whatever your goals, remember that they're yours alone; no one can change them for you. Need inspiration to divert from the beaten path of the marriage-minded? In *Savage Beauty*, a biography of the poet Edna St. Vincent Millay, author Nancy Milford conveys that Millay's goals for dating were essentially to provide her with material for her poetry on love. So, intent on her goal, Millay became an expert dater, flirt, and all-around man magnet, despite the fact that she was both obsessively self-critical and fearful of others (classic symptoms of a shy person).

Setting Short-Term Goals

To help your future dreams materialize, you'll need to set manageable, short-term goals that are measurable and specific, such as: "I'll attend a local singles' function once a month." If you're focused only on your long-term goal, you'll become frustrated because it's too far in the future. I've had clients tell me their long-term goal is to find "the one"—that person who is fated to share their destiny. Yet they have no idea how to help themselves achieve that goal today or tomorrow. Zeroing in on such a target without interim steps is like being in college, knowing you'd like to be a doctor but without taking biology and chemistry classes. Not only is it frustrating, it's counterproductive. The insistent "I want it now" desire can sabotage your step-by-step efforts and make you appear needy or desperate.

COACH'S CORNER

Organized athletics are an excellent vehicle to place a shy person in a social context, because the boundaries are clear and everyone knows what he or she is supposed to do. You have an immediate role, which is to be a team player. The shy often shine on teams because they conform, they're not sore losers, and they play hard. Typically, they're excellent teammates—and that's a flattering platform for meeting others.

If you're painfully shy, your first goal might be as basic as "I want to show up" at whatever dating event or social situation you'd like to attend. Then, eventually, expand to "I want to show up and talk with one or two people." To succeed, break dating projects down into small, manageable half- or mini-steps and be persistent. You'll be surprised how much progress you can make by continuing to inch forward.

Suppose you've decided that you want to be married by age thirty-five. What, then, do you do today, tomorrow, and next week to help you work toward your stated dream? (This becomes similar to tackling a big project at work.) Your first steps might be to join an organization where potential eligible partners can be found. You could take tango lessons, join a church or synagogue group, a ski club, a hiking group, or any other organization where you can attend regularly, enjoy the activity, and possibly meet your life partner—or at least potential dates. The immediate objective could be, for example, to participate in a team sport or join a book club.

What are your immediate dating goals? If you like, write them in the space on page 36.

My short-term goals for dating are:

Setting objectives for your personal life is important because you need a "carrot" in the near future. If, for example, you want a life partner, that's the motivation you need to get out there. It's no different than saying you want to own your own home instead of renting and networking to find a better-paying job to achieve it. But learning how to run the race your way and accomplishing each measurable goal can boost your motivation and dating endurance.

WHAT'S YOUR COURAGE SCORE?

We complete this chapter with your baseline courage score. On a scale of 1 to 10, with 1 being the courage of a kitten (you rarely leave your house and don't date much), and 10 the courage of a lion (you go out often and feel at ease in many different situations), rate your initial courage score. How generally courageous do you feel today? Circle your score below.

1 1.5 2 2.5 3 3.5 4 4.5 5 5.5 6 6.5 7 7.5 8 8.5 9 9.5 10

You may wish to write your score in the space that follows: _____

If your courage score is more kitten than lion—perhaps it's 1—the techniques in this book will help you gradually increase it in small, manageable increments. We'll revisit the concept of the courage score at the end of every chapter to help you monitor your progress. With knowledge of your dating pattern in tow, you're already off to a solid start, especially if you think of other people—perhaps even family members—who are in the dark and controlled by their shyness. In general, when it comes to managing shyness, there's nothing that produces courage more than self-awareness.

{THREE}

THE SHYNESS ATTACK, STAGE ONE:
FEAR OF INITIATION

MICHAEL, A THIRTY-FIVE-YEAR-OLD PHYSICIAN, once asked me, "Am I the biggest loser or what?" He said it facetiously to the group, but it was obvious his experience at a recent dinner party had caused him a lot of pain. "After I gave the hostess a bouquet of fresh daisies, she took my arm and stepped with me into her cavernous living room to make introductions. It was like 'the eligible doctor's here, everyone.' I hate being singled out because of my profession," Michael said. "And when I looked around the room at the clusters of really pretty women, I could literally feel and hear my heart pounding. They all looked so cool and confident. Then a thought crept into my head: 'Why would anyone want to talk to me?' No matter how many initials you put behind my name, I'll never feel like I'm part of the in-crowd," he said.

Alison, a twenty-six-year-old jewelry designer, nodded. "The other night, I was sitting in my theater seat just dying to reach over and take Peter's hand. It was our second date, and I

38

thought it would be okay because he'd had his arm around me earlier. But I just couldn't do it. If he pulled his hand away, I'd be devastated. So I just sat there, hoping he'd make a move." (He finally did halfway into the performance they were watching.)

Michael and Alison are just two workshop participants who were often caught in the throes of the first stage of a shyness attack, the fear of initiation. The shyness attack is a phenomenon I recognized as a common thread among my clients. What Michael and Alison described was a specific type of fear that has kept them from making the first move—to say hello, to make conversation, to take a hand, to catch the eye of someone they were interested in, or even to ask someone out.

Maybe you know it well. On the surface, it's the fear of being rejected, of encountering others' disinterest, dislike, or even disgust. But feelings of incompetence and inadequacy—a deep concern that you just don't measure up—make up the core of this distress. When the fear of initiation grips you, you automatically hesitate, or even retreat (perhaps by leaving the party or canceling the date), and thereby miss opportunities to meet and possibly connect with others.

Of the three stages of a shyness attack, fear of initiation is the starting gate. Passing through that gate is critical for gaining control so that you can master many of the aspects of dating that require you to put yourself out there—like approaching someone who interests you and introducing yourself—or lovingly taking a hand. Let's face it. Making that first move can be scary. You risk rejection and humiliation. No one wants to feel like a fool. As you learn to deal with the fear of initiation, in time the important first-impression and introductory period of any meeting or social interaction will become less loaded. When you start to manage the fear—for example, plucking up the courage to introduce yourself at a party and chat with people—you'll accumulate a series of victories that become the successful history you can draw upon to remind yourself: *I did it at the party last weekend. I can do it again.*

Not every introductory situation will go smoothly, however. You may ask a man to dance who says no. You may post a message on an online dating service and get few responses. No matter—it happens to everyone. As you become attuned to the fear and learn to accept it, work with it, and outmaneuver it, you'll be less vulnerable to uncomfortable feelings, such as shame and embarrassment, that can thwart your progress. You'll be better able to dust yourself off and start again. The other stages of a shyness attack will also lose their power over you. But it all starts by taking small steps to gain control of stage one.

RECOGNIZING THE FEAR

Dealing successfully with dating-related shyness requires awareness of this initial fear. How do you know when the fear of initiation has you in its grasp? In some cases, you can't avoid the signals because the onset is physiological and dramatic, encompassing the typical fight-or-flight response. For instance, suppose you're at brunch with a roomful of strangers or in a movie theater on a second date—or perhaps simply thinking about meeting someone new, going to the party, or being on that date—but you react as if you're standing in the middle of Madison Avenue in the path of an oncoming bus. Your sympathetic nervous system revs up and your heart gallops. Your palms sweat. Your pupils dilate, and your breathing becomes shallow. The message: Your personal safety is threatened. Danger! Get out of the way! That's fear of initiation at its most visceral.

In its more subtle forms, the fear of initiation can mask itself as resentment, depression, anger, or exhaustion. At the party, Dr. Michael said he hesitated to join in any of the conversations already in play (until, fortunately, someone asked him a question) because "I was tired and I had too many things on my mind from working all week." Yet, Michael knew that wasn't entirely true. He admitted that he had had the energy to attend the event; he had gotten dressed and painstakingly chosen just the right clothes. He'd even bought a new pair of shoes. He wasn't exhausted; rather, he was afraid of entering the room and making his presence known.

Sally, a fifty-two-year-old artist, hides behind her fear by masking it as resentment over our culture's obsession with youth. "There's no possibility for me to meet men close to my own age because they want thirty-year-olds. So I spend every waking hour with my sculptures. They don't make me feel like an old has-been," she said. Similarly, Griffin, a forty-one-year-old lawyer, hides behind depression. He sleeps at least ten hours a day and never leaves his bed on Saturday. "I just realized that putting on my hearing aids, which I've worn since childhood (due to a congenital hearing defect) is such a downer, I'd rather sleep the day away. I'm so self-conscious about people having to accommodate for my disability that I'd rather not socialize," he said. And Evelyn, a sixty-year-old widow, seethed when she described how, now that she is without a husband, no one ever calls or asks her for dinner. Why doesn't she phone some of her old friends? "I don't want to bother them," she replied.

Besides exhaustion, resentment, anger, or depression, the fear of initiation can also camouflage itself as self-blame. Often, I hear clients give excuses for being mere spectators at parties and other social, meet-people events. Marie, a thirty-four-year-old pediatrician, said, "I'm so average looking. And besides, I work too many odd hours. I'm sure there's no one who can deal with that." Others have said: "I'm sure my life is so boring compared to hers." "I wouldn't be of interest to anyone." "He wouldn't like me anyway." So they hang back and wait for someone to approach them and do the hard work of breaking the ice. Sure, that's one way to go about it, but to continually take this passive stance reinforces the fear and is not nearly as proactive and confidence building as doing it yourself.

Another manifestation of the fear of initiation is blaming the other person. Many of my shy singles let the passing parade of prospects slip by because others "prevent" them from making their presence known. "I couldn't get a word in. No one gave me time to talk—that's why I was so quiet," said Joseph, a divorced father of two, who had been trying to meet someone through singles events at his church. The fear of initiation was the likely subtext.

WHY GROUP ACTIVITIES CAN BE A LIFELINE

Certainly, you can meet someone at work, by going online, or through a network of friends and relatives. But many of the shy singles in my workshops feel especially comfortable meeting others through organized group activities, such as taking a course on a subject they enjoy or enrolling in an exercise class. A group activity can take the edge off the fear of initiation because you have a built-in subject (the class) for conversation. Even if you don't meet anyone special, it's good practice to mingle.

When Sheila, one of my shy clients, came to me for the first time three years ago, I suggested that she become a student. She debated for weeks about what kind of class to enroll in. Ultimately, she decided on salsa dance lessons at a continuing education university. After recruiting a friend to go with her, she was hooked after only two sessions. Salsa became Sheila's sport, so to speak, and she began looking for other places that offered salsa throughout New York City. "I'm even considering taking a salsa dancing cruise through the Panama Canal," Sheila bubbled. Salsa has been fantastic for Sheila because it's so organized. "Everybody dances and you keep switching partners, so you get to automatically meet lots of people," she relayed. Once Sheila became familiar with salsa and its routine, she began going to lessons by herself. She hasn't met anyone special yet, but she's no longer sitting at home alone in her apartment. She's found a social venue that works for her.

This fear has many guises, but one common denominator: It keeps you from feeling confident, relaxed, and able to present the real you. Of course, there are some days when you're honestly not up for attending the party or going on that set-up date—or meeting anyone new, for that matter. Everyone has those days. You may be too exhausted from work, your schedule, or your rigorous regimen at the gym. You may not be in the mood for chitchat, or maybe you really do have the flu or a stomachache. But if you frequently use these sorts of reasons to avoid social events, then you probably do suffer from the fear of initiation.

GETTING A GRIP ON IT

It's time to wrestle your way to freedom. If you embrace defeat and don't fight your way out, you accept a life characterized by retreat—and that is spiritually depleting. Deep down, you want to be recognized for who you are. We all do. As Tara, another shy single, said, "I don't want to be the star of anything. I just don't want to hide in plain sight." How universally true. If you're like Tara and other Shys, you want to introduce yourself and get to know who is out there. It comes from the part in all of us that craves the pleasures of active participation. And you sense you *can* greet others at a party, sign up with an online dating service, or go out for drinks after work. You just know it. But you have to do it your way. Perhaps you may never get past stage one and become "the life of the party." Flirting may never be your forte. But there's a lot of wiggle room between such ambitious aspirations and being invisible! Managing stage one is to stand fast rather than run away. To say "Here I am" in some fashion, to someone.

Take a moment now to assess when you experience the fear of initiation. On page 44, write down three memorable situations where your head said go and your heart said no.

1. _____

   _____

   _____

   _____

2. _____

   _____

   _____

   _____

3. _____

   _____

   _____

   _____

Based on what you've written above, what's your verdict? Do you note any similarities among your fear of initiation experiences? If so, write your thoughts below by completing the statement, "The fear of initiation often overcomes me when . . ." (Examples: I get into bed with him. I enter a large party. I sit across from her at the restaurant. I'm sitting at a dinner with twelve others.)

_____

_____

_____

_____

_____

_____

SMALL STEPS TO MANAGE STAGE ONE

Once you have arrived at a better understanding of stage one by naming the types of situations in which you most frequently encounter it, you can begin to develop an action plan for managing this problem—one small step at a time. "Once I realized this was my personal challenge, I started looking for ways to practice acquiring my new 'skill,'" said Kay, a shy attorney in private practice. "Now, I go on dates set up by good friends and force myself to attend networking cocktail parties every week or so. You never know when or how you're going to meet someone interesting, and I don't want to miss out on my chances to practice." To help yourself face the fear of initiation, consider the following steps.

Step One: Self-Acceptance

Repeat this mantra: *I have a fear of initiation and I can reduce its power step by step.* Chances are, this fear has been with you for a long time. It's part of your personality. You can't make it disappear overnight. But by accepting the fear, you'll stop spinning your wheels, wasting time, energy, and emotion futilely willing your shyness away. This may sound counterintuitive, but as your dating coach, I know you can trust me on this one. The sooner you accept the fear, the more easily and comfortably you'll manage your shyness and stop a full-blown attack in its tracks. When you feel the fear coming on during any specific event, or even if you're just thinking about being at an event, it pays to say something like, "Hello, fear of initiation. There you are again." (Some of my clients even give their fear a pet name.) By naming it and welcoming it, the fear will lose steam; it will be less apt to overpower how you think, act, and feel. Try it for yourself.

Step Two: Mindset Makeover

You can influence how you perceive your "fear of initiation" experience to reduce the threat to your personal safety. Remember the fight-or-flight response. Tell yourself, *I can think about my problem in a new way.* This cognitive shift can help change your behavior so that initiating feels more comfortable.

Below are several examples of cognitive shifts I frequently ask my workshop participants to make to help them stop the panic.

- **Repeat silently, *I'm not alone.*** If you're a shy single, you probably think you're the only one. But remember that millions of us—nearly half the adult population—label ourselves as shy. And according to census statistics, more than 50 percent of the population is single, so the combination of these two categories suggests a very large group of people who share the two umbrellas of the shy single with you. Doubtless, at any social event you attend, you'll have company. By considering the probability that you're not the only shy person there, you'll feel less vulnerable, isolated, and self-conscious. Want proof?

  The next time you're at a party, take a moment to notice others in the room who aren't initiating or engaging in conversation. Perhaps it's the woman by the bar or even your new date. Remember Alison in the theater who was too frightened to express warmth towards her date, even though he had already shown affection for her? She admitted that she couldn't imagine that Peter could have his own fears and possibly be shy, too. It's classic for shyness sufferers to perceive an interaction only through the prism of their perspective. Alison thought, 'If Peter wanted to hold hands, he'd do it. What's wrong with me?' It never occurred to Alison that Peter might hesitate because he was worried about being rejected if he made the first move. Coming to that realization was an *ah-ha* moment for Alison that made her less self-critical.

  Similarly, when you're at a party or on a date, the value of what you do or say isn't usually foremost on the minds of others, but rather how they appear to you, as well as those around them. Let's face it. We're a self-absorbed lot, we imperfect humans. The woman you meet at the party would also like to be thought of as witty and charming; the man you just responded to online could be worrying that you think he's boring. You're not the only self-conscious person here. Others also worry about how they're perceived. Reminding yourself of those two realities can loosen the grip the fear of initiation has on you.

- **Think, *I'm helping others.*** If you initiate a conversation or an introduction, you'll help others feel more comfortable and feel good about themselves. After all, it's flattering to be approached and a relief to someone else when you take that first step. "I've always been altruistic, perhaps even to a fault," said Anne, a shy single who enjoys volunteering at a neighborhood rescue center for abandoned cats. "Once I realized that being proactive made others feel more comfortable, the whole introductory process became much easier. I've got it down. I simply stick out my hand and say, 'Hi, I'm Anne. And you are?'"

- **Put yourself in others' shoes.** Shy singles often don't realize how unapproachable they can appear to others. Angry, sad, snobbish, intimidating, rude, unhappy, bored, and aloof are just a few of the adjectives my clients report being labeled by others. Can you imagine? When you're afraid of initiating because it looks as if others are indifferent to you—they see you standing against the wall, for example, and don't approach you—it could be because they think you prefer it that way. Likewise, by hanging back, you could be sending stay-away signals. "It's funny, but William thought I wanted to hover next to the potato chip bowl all night," said Amy, a formerly shy single, speaking of her husband and how they first met. "If he hadn't come up and made a joke about it, I'm sure I would have polished off the entire bowl out of nervousness."

- **Take a "no one cares" attitude.** Shys are often so self-conscious at the initiation stage, they feel the room close in on them. "Whenever I go to a cocktail party, I feel like I'm making my appearance on the red carpet at the Academy Awards," said Kathleen, a commercial property manager. "I'd better look great and say something witty—or else my 'career' as a social being is over." What tremendous pressure we place on ourselves! The truth is, with the possible exception of a hostess who would enjoy herself more if you mingled, no one cares if you don't initiate conversation. You're not on the red carpet. You're not standing on stage with an audience waiting for you to speak so the play can begin. Look around at the gathering. Taking a step back and putting yourself in perspective can ease the burden of making that first bold move. As you'll see, life goes on without you.

Step Three: Walk the Walk

Okay, so you've accepted your fear of initiation. You're starting to see things as they are rather than through your previously self-centered perspective. You're beginning to make the cognitive shifts that allow you to think differently about yourself and stopping the habits that interfere with your functioning. As your dating coach, I can tell you that initiating is sometimes easier said than done. Still, here are twelve strategies for you to consider trying.

Read through the twelve tactics that follow, then rank them in order of difficulty, 1 being the easiest you can imagine yourself doing—the activity you're most willing to try—and 12 the most challenging, the biggest stretch for your shyness management skills. This ranking will be used to calibrate your courage score, which we'll discuss at the end of the chapter.

1. **Rehearse.** Before an event like a cocktail party, role-play. Imagine yourself, for example, walking over to a small group, smiling, and saying something friendly like, "Hello, I'm Jane's downstairs neighbor." Then visualize someone in the crowd sticking out her hand and saying, "Hi. I know her from work. This is a great building. You live in a similar apartment?" You stand the best chance of enjoying the interaction if you can preview it in your mind. But keep your script easy; your "lines" should be as simple as saying hi, your name, and, for example, how you know the host/hostess. Don't attempt anything too ambitious at first—like trying to tell a hugely funny joke. This is for extroverts with a great memory and skilled timing. Remember that people appreciate simple, straightforward gestures, such as saying your name, asking for theirs, and reaching for a handshake.

   But it also pays to be prepared in case you're rebuffed. If you feel slighted, perhaps by a sour look or humorless response, keep in mind that it may have nothing to do with what you said or did. We all bring our own histories to an encounter. No matter how clever or nice you are, the man you choose to speak to may be worried or stressed about something that happened earlier. Your date may be nervous or tense from work. A less-than-enthusiastic reception could be entirely unrelated to you, especially if you don't know the person. Imagine yourself walking over to a small group and being met with an unfriendly welcome; if that happens, smile at them, move on, and say to yourself, *Good. I got that over with. Next!*

RANK _____

2. **Look and act approachable.** Think about keeping your face relaxed. If necessary, practice how this looks in a mirror before the event. If you stand with your arms folded or wrapped around your body, you can appear defensive and "closed." Standing off to the side or spending an entire date leaning back in your chair can send off-limits signals. Rather, lean forward slightly when you speak to express your interest to convey that you're very much a part of the conversation.

RANK _____

3. **Wear a conversation starter.** This tip is a little daring, but try wearing something catchy that's still true to your style, but which others are bound to comment on, like an unusual brooch, a quirky tie, a whimsical skirt, a funky handbag, or even just a fun color. I'm not suggesting you walk over to someone and say, "Would you look at this?" But it does increase the chances that others will notice what you're wearing and say, "Oh, that's great. Where did you get it?" Be ready to answer questions about it.

RANK _____

4. **Be prepared.** It's a twist on the old Boy Scouts motto, but being conversationally prepared with a topic before a social event is often a compelling way to capture someone's interest and ease your way past the initiation stage. Read the newspaper or tune into the news before you arrive at the party. You'll have something interesting to say that could spark a conversation or comment. Or, make a mental list of subjects you're comfortable broaching. Think about what you'd like to say concerning movies or books you've enjoyed or disliked, restaurants you've tried, hobbies you've recently taken up, or insights about business or the economy. You'll be armed with introductory material and conversational connectors in case there's a lull. You can also ask questions to get the ball rolling, such as, "What did you think of that X news item in the *Times* today?" Be ready to jump in during unexpected downtime.

   RANK _____

5. **Delay your reaction.** At a party or other social event, take a moment to give the room a global glance and size up who might be a good match for you. You do have the option of not engaging right away. Carol, a human resources executive in her mid-fifties, loathed parties. After several workshops, she still disliked them, especially when she had to introduce herself. But she learned the tricks for breaking the ice I've mentioned here, and use them she did—but only when she wanted to. She admitted that sometimes she simply permits herself to be an observer. "When I finally realized I didn't have to leap into a group to be at the party, I gave myself permission to sit back and watch and see who might be interesting for me to approach when I'm ready." Only when Carol was emotionally set to enter the fray did she step forward. In group situations, especially, the decision to wait and assess the scene can be as empowering as plunging in with an arsenal of icebreakers, be-

cause you know you're in control and that you can actively participate when you choose to and speak when you're ready.

RANK _____

6. **Use the buddy system.** Whether you're going to a party or even just out for coffee on a Saturday afternoon, it pays to travel with a trusted friend. A party pal can ease introductions and possibly linger until the conversation starts flowing. In fact, that's how one of my clients, Michelle, met her husband, Everett. She went to a mixer at a health club with a girlfriend, Emily, who happened to be rather outgoing. Emily approached Everett and they chatted a while. The two didn't click, but she was thoughtful enough to say, "Do you want to meet my friend, Michelle?" Three years later, Emily was the maid of honor at Michelle and Everett's wedding. While that kind of love connection doesn't happen every day, it does happen, and having a friend along can help pave the way. Because you'll automatically have someone to talk to, you'll feel less self-conscious and conspicuous.

RANK _____

7. **'Fess up.** Shyness doesn't have to be a secret. If you feel comfortable, go ahead and reveal it. But you needn't use the word "shy" to get your point across. "I'm not that comfortable in these situations" or "It's hard for me to talk with people I hardly know" or "I tend to be reserved at first" work just as well. What's the benefit of telling someone up front how you feel? Your tentativeness won't be mistaken for disinterest. And the more you can

COACH'S CORNER

If the person or group you connect with at a social event lacks chemistry, simply excuse yourself after several minutes to "refresh your drink," then try again with others. (If you have a full drink in hand and feel the need to escape, excuse yourself to go to the hors d'oeuvre spread or to make a phone call. You get the idea.)

put how you feel into words, the less you'll act it out. There's also the chance that the person you're talking to will say, "Me, too!" and voilà!—a conversation has started.

RANK _____

8. **Take conversational cues.** You're at a dinner party and you're seemingly dissimilar to everyone there. What to do? Consider yourself someone whose job it is to find a common denominator and enrich yourself. Ignore the cacophony in your head that says, 'Why am I here? What could I possibly talk about with these people? They're going to think I'm so boring.' Instead, give yourself permission to be quiet and listen for conversational cues that can spark dialogue. Try to hitch on to sound bites of party chitchat. "Did you say you were in Geneva last week? I was there years ago and thought it so beautiful. . . . "

RANK _____

9. **Fake it.** When you're entering a novel group situation, such as attending new classes, joining a church or a health club, starting a job, or even moving to a different city, play a game with yourself. Decide for one or two weeks to pretend you're not shy. You could imitate someone whose social style you admire, although you probably have a general idea of how the nonshy act: They smile a lot; they walk up to people; they laugh at jokes, participate with animation, and easily suggest that "everyone go out for a drink later on!" Countless participants in my workshops report that if they frame the task by saying to themselves, "I'm going to play a role for a limited time," they actually break through barriers, avert a shyness attack, and readily make friends.

RANK _____

10. **Use the environment as a prop.** To ignite conversation, pay attention to your surroundings, and employ them to jump-start dialogue. If you're at work, which can be a natural place to meet someone, you could ask about a colleague's background: "So, have you always been in information technology?" You're browsing at a bookstore and you happen to catch someone's eye: "Oh, I've been meaning to check out that book. How is it?" is a perfect beginning. You're in a restaurant, sitting with a group of friends, and you notice a cute guy at the next table: "Excuse me, but I see you ordered the seared tuna. How is it?"

     RANK _____

11. **Tell a story.** Select one about yourself or someone you know that relates in some way to your surroundings, current events, or the conversational topic at hand. You can do this to fill a lull in the conversation, change the subject, or simply get everyone talking. Revealing something about yourself will make others warm to you. Although spontaneous stories are helpful, there's no harm in having a self-revelatory story in mind to call upon if you tend to have trouble thinking on your feet. If being self-revelatory or forthcoming doesn't come easily, rehearse your "stock" story so you'll feel more confident when the time comes. You don't have to be funny or overly dramatic. Your anecdote just has to have a beginning, middle, and end.

     RANK _____

12. **Do your homework.** If you're invited to a party and you're comfortable with the host/hostess, inquire about the other guests before the event. Ask for details, such as how they know the host/hostess, then formulate questions and have topics in mind to discuss when party time comes. To establish common ground, think of an experience or two in your

own life that might parallel the lives of these people. If you feel embarrassed about making this reconnaissance, keep in mind that several moments of discomfort now may help you avoid several hours of distress later. Here are a few questions worth asking: "Who do you think would be especially interesting for me to talk to? Will anyone at the party be in the same line of work? Would you mind introducing me to that person?" Then, when you're at the party, scan the scene for details to guide your actions. Direct your focus outward; observe others and listen actively.

RANK _____

YOUR ACTION PLAN

The twelve behavioral strategies listed on pages 48–53 involve interfacing with others. Like the four cognitive shifts I mentioned on pages 46–47, they'll be part of your action plan to manage dating shyness and increase your courage.

To tackle the fear of initiation, when you're out socially begin to experiment with your number-one-ranked strategy. Do it several times until it comes naturally to you, then proceed to your number-two-ranked strategy, and so on. If an action seems too difficult to tackle, you can give yourself half a point on your courage score for just visualizing yourself doing this behavior prior to an anxiety-producing event. (Even that takes courage.) After visualizing, spend as little as five minutes practicing it with other people once you're ready. Of course, you must eventually force yourself to try whatever step seems especially challenging, but you will build courage one small step at a time.

Which strategies will you try? Record your game plan in the space that follows. Writing it down makes it real—and more committed to memory. Consider photocopying this page for easy reference when you're in the dating trenches. Some of my shy singles even post their written strategies in a place where they can see them often until the techniques become second nature.

I'd like to try to manage my shyness by:

_____

_____

_____

_____

_____

_____

_____

_____

_____

_____

_____

_____

_____

_____

_____

_____

It Gets Easier

Overcoming the fear of initiation sounds like a lot of work, doesn't it? Take heart. As you break through your shyness barrier and begin to initiate more often, you'll be amply rewarded. Although your shyness may never disappear altogether, the tenor of it will change. It will lose its ability to dominate the moment. In time, you'll find yourself able to draw on your considerable strengths and experience to repeatedly present your best self to others with less effort, because confidence will become part of your personal history. "My shyness is on a different level," said Julie, thirty-five, a banker who worked hard for nearly a year to manage her shyness. Eventually, she began dating someone seriously. "My timidity hasn't completely dissipated, but I can definitely manage it better. It's not so much of an impediment anymore. It's just another part of me." It is possible to develop new emotional muscles that will get stronger each time you use them—if you believe you can. "I'm amazed at how much better I am at just talking to new people," said James, an investment analyst. "It's like I've trained for a marathon and now, I'm just running."

When You Just Want to Hide

Because shy singles are often saddled with mega self-consciousness, they're often awash with reasons to avoid others or not be seen. "I look terrible." "I don't know what to say." "I'm

---

SHOULD YOU BREAK FOR SPEED DATING?

These days, with the expansion of the nine-to-five workweek and countless other factors, it can be tough to find the time and energy to meet someone. To compensate, several organizations have initiated the concept of the three-to-ten-minute "speed date." Maybe you've heard of it. With this method of quickie coupling, you spend an evening mini-dating a multitude of men or women in minute increments before a buzzer goes off—next!

While it sounds like a catchy idea, it may not be for you if you're shy around new people and need time to warm up. Three to ten minutes may simply not be enough time to find your dating legs or give you a sense of whether you're interested in the other person. On the other hand, some Shys like the venue because it's so refreshingly structured. "It's nice to be in a roomful of people who all want to meet someone," said Erika, a fashion editor who describes herself as chatty but shy. "But I have no clue how to get my game on, which is why it works for me. Somebody else brings the men; I just have to talk."

To find out about speed dating, or something similar, in your area, watch for ads in your local newspaper or type "speed dating" into your computer's search engine.

too nervous, unhappy, moody, or tired to be much fun." "Work is wiping me out." Sound familiar? Of course, if you consistently cave in to these feelings and limit going out, you won't learn how to manage your shyness by doing. (Experience is the greatest teacher.) With the aid of the strategies I've described, attempted one by one, you will assertively confront your fear of initiation.

Still, there will be times—many times—when you just want to take a vacation from the whole thing. You'll be out, but you'd rather be home with a cup of tea and a good book. Or maybe you'll see someone you've met before, but it's a bad mood/hair/clothes day and you'd rather take cover or dart across the street to avoid contact. Or you look around a room and think, 'You know, I'm feeling shy and the truth is, I've had a rough day and I don't feel like fighting past these feelings right now.' So go ahead and flee. It's absolutely okay. "When I go out a lot—to several events after work and to something on Friday and Saturday night, I know I'm headed for some downtime," said Daniel, a retail salesperson. "Sometimes, you just need to recharge."

For the shy and nonshy alike, being "out" requires energy and the right frame of mind. The key is to realize you have options—to go home or go out, to stay at the party or not, to meet up with someone you've agreed to meet or cancel. Just knowing that can be freeing. And by all means, if you're having an off day, go ahead and give yourself permission to exit the courage campaign. Sometimes, even the most confident do that because they just don't feel like sharing themselves. We all need to take a breather now and then.

WHAT'S YOUR COURAGE SCORE?

We complete this chapter with your courage score. On a scale of 1 to 10, with 1 being the courage of a kitten (you rarely go out and contribute little when you're out socially), and 10 the courage of a lion (you approach others at parties; you ask someone for a date), rate your fear of initiation courage score. Circle your score below.

1 1.5 **2** 2.5 **3** 3.5 **4** 4.5 **5** 5.5 **6** 6.5 **7** 7.5 **8** 8.5 **9** 9.5 **10**

You may wish to write your score in the space that follows: _____

If your courage score is more kitten than lion—perhaps it's 1.5—ask yourself what you can incorporate from your action plans to increase your score to a 2. For a .5 courage score increase, for example, you might introduce yourself to just one person at every event you attend for the next month. Since you've now identified how your shyness manifests itself and when, as well as having an action plan, you have the tools you need to increase your courage score one small increment at a time.

When you experience the fear of initiation, recalculate your courage score. Try to raise it another half point by attempting—or even imagining—one of the cognitive and/or behavioral courage steps suggested in your action plan. Keep in mind that courage is consistently putting one foot in front of the other. As you take on more and more of these exercises, you will see your score gradually improve. With each small, managed step, you generate the reinforcing emotion called hope and a buoyant sense of increasing confidence.

"You must do the thing you think you cannot do."
— *Eleanor Roosevelt, 1960*

{FOUR}

THE SHYNESS ATTACK, STAGE TWO: CIRCUIT OVERLOAD

PATTI, A TWENTY-EIGHT-YEAR-OLD investment analyst, recalled one night how she'd smiled at the handsome man with deep blue eyes. They were at a bar on the New Jersey shore. "Hello," she said. "I'm Patti." She extended her hand and shook his confidently. He grinned back. 'That went well', she thought. 'I'm getting better at introducing myself.' But from there, things went downhill. "Do you live near here?" he asked. "No," Patti replied, feeling herself begin to stiffen. She looked around the room, groping for something more to say. "I've practically been coming to this bar forever," he offered expectantly. Patti looked at the floor and said nothing. 'He's going to think I'm boring,' she thought. "My temples throbbed. I couldn't think. 'That's nice,' was all I could muster," she said.

Patti was in the throes of the second stage of a shyness attack: overload. It had been the theme of several of our sessions together. Patti was definitely getting better at pushing through stage one of a shyness attack, but stage two had stumped her. How did she take an introduction to the next step and actually carry on a conversation, one that flowed, gathered momentum, and made her feel like she was connecting? It sounded so simple, but faced with a person she wanted to talk to, her courage failed. The good news is there are concrete tools you can use to work through the mental roadblocks of this stage.

BLOWING AN EMOTIONAL FUSE

During the first stage of a shyness attack you feel so over-whelmed and paralyzed by potential rejection and uncertainty that you can't make the first move. Anxiety and the anticipated judgments of others overwhelm your conscious thoughts. If you're shy with strangers, stage one may make you hesitate to go out socially. At stage two, self-consciousness is a continuing theme. Perhaps you've forced yourself to take that first step by leaving your house or saying hello or putting your hand on your lover's belly, but then you feel paralyzed. You lose your ability to go with the flow, to speak fluidly, or behave easily. Often you can't even think. You may even feel as if you can't move a muscle. Meanwhile, a litany of silent self-reproach ('I'm so blah' or 'I'm uninteresting') or defensive anger ('No one gives a damn about me' or 'They all think they're so smart') churns in your mind.

The approach/avoidance associated with stage two conflicts with your natural desire to connect. Even though you've shown up (which is a laudable feat in itself), you simply can't summon the ability to casually converse because your emotions and thoughts conspire against you. As a result, your cleverness, intel-ligence, and sexiness get pushed to the side. During this stage, a so-called pleasurable social experience, like getting to know someone at a dinner party, can become, in a word, stressful.

Stage two is a particularly perplexing component of a shyness attack because it can occur despite your success with making the first move. Let's say, for example, you now recognize the fear of initiation when it strikes. You've come to accept it and realize that you're not the only one who suffers from shyness. And you're using some of the tactics I suggested in chapter three to help yourself think and act more constructively when you first meet someone. Even still, you can then be sideswiped by stage two and all its complexities. It can strike when you're "connecting"—when you're exchanging information and trying to get to know someone a little better (and they you). The frustration of wanting to say or do something more, but feeling self-conscious and blocked, leads to overload.

Stage two manifests itself in various ways. Many of my clients tend to categorize themselves as either a "freezer" or a "flooder," although some are both; which dominates depends on the situation. Some overloaded Shys shut down (freeze) when they're in the middle of a shyness attack. Others begin jabbering (aka flooding) after the initial hellos have worn off. They say too much in the opening minutes, such as their desire for two or more children, preferably within the next three years, the fact they want a cat, or that they like to clean their apartment in the nude. That sort of thing. And the more they think someone is willing to listen, the more the floodgates open. Some Shys may do one or the other. "I can freeze or I can flood. It sometimes just depends on how receptive or even how attractive I find the other person," said Patrick, a shy single in his early thirties. Despite having a particularly tough time managing stage two, he could still poke fun at himself about it with the group.

WHAT HAPPENS DURING STAGE TWO

Like stage one, there's a physiological undercurrent driving stage two; this one rests with the feel-good brain chemical serotonin. When you're in the throes of stage two, the theory is that serotonin doesn't get absorbed efficiently by the appropriate receptors. Because there isn't enough serotonin within your brain cells to calm you at that moment, your thoughts and feelings overload, and anxiety skyrockets.

Coupled with circuit overload's anxiety are feelings of disappointment and self-consciousness, which can make this stage particularly frustrating. A Greek chorus of self-doubt buries whatever thoughts you'd love to express. When you're suffering from the parallel and irreconcilable conversations going on in your mind during stage two, you don't believe you can present a "self" that others will respond to positively. You turn inward, and by doing so, you forgo opportunities to use the handy environmental cues right in front of you to counteract this nervous moment.

Like stage one, stage two may be accompanied by physical symptoms, such as a racing heart and a strained facial expression, which could be the only clues that you're uncomfortable. Oddly, your body can require huge amounts of energy to remain in what appears to be mental and physical stillness. But if it's any consolation, keep in mind that while the surplus of emotional and physical sensations that define stage two of a shyness attack feels awful, it may be invisible to others. Unless you look scared enough for others to pay attention, no one but you will probably know how anxious you feel.

Freezing

Many Shys say that during stage two, they feel tongue-tied, boring, frightened, and confused. "It's like I'm in the 'hot seat,'" said Brian, a thirty-two-year-old consultant for a large marketing firm. "I worry about saying the wrong thing, being laughed at, misunderstood, attacked, or worse, being ignored or brushed off." When you're unsure of what to say or do, you shut down and live up to your own worst potential, which can fuel your fears for future events. Mary, a thirty-seven-year-old trial attorney who liked attending dance parties throughout New York City as her principal way to "get out there," said, "When I'm in stage two, I can't think of anything to say other than 'nice band' or 'I like the music.' Then, my mind blanks, my throat constricts, and my face gets red. Sometimes, I even start to giggle, like I'm in the sixth grade, or something. When that sort of thing happens, I want to run from the room and never go out again." Many others in the workshop nodded as Mary spoke. She had struck a resonant chord. *If you don't learn to manage stage two, it can manage you.*

Flooding

Another component of circuit overload is flooding. This may be even more familiar to you than the resounding silence or heightened self-consciousness associated with freezing. As with freezing, you've passed stage one—perhaps to the satisfaction of your inner critic, perhaps not—and put yourself out there. You've entered the party. Maybe you're on a first date, or maybe you've just met someone intriguing and gone past the "Hello, I'm so-and-so" phase. Then stage two steps in, but instead of withholding your thoughts, the floodgates open almost reflexively and a deluge of words bursts forth. In short, you do the opposite of a freezer: You talk—a lot. And while your "audience" may relish your conversational generosity—at first—they can also grow restless if you don't invite them to contribute. (After all, everyone wants to be heard.) It can also become embarrassing if, afterward, you feel you revealed too much about yourself too quickly.

Flooders may or may not self-monitor their input with swirling thoughts about their performance, such as, 'Maybe I shouldn't have said that. Why am I telling her about my grandmother's operation? Why do I still feel like an adolescent when I'm thirty-five? Oh, he probably thinks I'm a ditz.' Marla, a shy copy editor, said, "I was at a cocktail party full of television types who seemed so confident and sophisticated. But there I was, stuck in stage two. After I said 'Hello, I'm Marla,' I started babbling, going on and on about how my puppy was doing with the potty training and how I had had a fight with my boss that afternoon—whatever popped into my head. I was mortified, but I couldn't stop myself." If babbling occurs in an intimate situation, the interruption can be taxing on you as well as your partner.

There's Hope

Whether you're a freezer or a flooder (or on occasion, one or the other), you probably know how challenging stage two can become. And that's my message to you: If you're prone to either freezing or flooding, you can, with practice, evolve into an engaging conversationalist who tells amusing or interesting anecdotes and leaves room for others to share theirs. You can also become a sensitive lover if the bedroom is where shyness strikes. (More on that in chapter nine.)

To help you determine how you experience circuit overload, take a moment now to assess what form stage two typically takes for you—and when you encounter this debilitating stage. For example, do you start stammering, or clamming up, right after the initial introduction, or a few minutes into a conversation, after the hellos have worn off? Write down three situations in which you either couldn't speak after introducing yourself or found yourself saying more than you intended once you got "the floor."

I think freezing or flooding may happen to me in the following situations:

1. _____

_____

_____

_____

_____

2. _____

_____

_____

_____

_____

3. _____

_____

_____

_____

_____

Based on what you've written above, what's your verdict? Do you note any similarities among your overload experiences? If so, write your thoughts below by completing the statement: *Circuit overload often overcomes me when:*

_____

_____

_____

_____

_____

SMALL, COGNITIVE SHIFTS
TO MANAGE STAGE TWO

Whether you're prone to freezing or flooding, the first step to managing this maddening stage is to surrender with compassion to the physical, emotional, and/or conversational reaction it brings. Fighting it by criticizing yourself or giving in to it and fleeing the scene will only feed your discomfort and deepen the ineptness you feel. Here are two empowering exercises to try.

1. Name stage two while it's happening. The ability to tell yourself that you're experiencing stage two and its associated, involuntary inhibition (or exhibition, if you flood) is extremely liberating. In psychology, it's called developing "an

observing ego," which means that while you're experiencing an overwhelming, intense emotional moment, you're simultaneously detaching from it—or as I characterize it, standing on stage and sitting in the audience at the same time. Living fully in the moment while also observing how you and others behave will give you a tremendous edge. One of my shy single clients, Kendrick, an actor, described how he plays the name game. "When I feel stage two coming on, I tell myself, 'Ah-ha. There you are, Stage Two, trying to sneak up on me. Let it be known. I know you're there.'"

To help minimize the stress of a freezing or flooding moment, choose a way to name it so that it resonates with you. Some Shys, such as Kendrick, prefer to personify the stage and talk to it. Others like to simply say to themselves, "I'm in circuit overload" or "I'm experiencing stage two, but it's going to be okay."

2. Remind yourself that stage two will pass. After you become aware that it is upon you, tell yourself that the paralysis you're feeling or the babbling you're experiencing is fleeting. And, indeed, it will be because you're going to dissipate it with awareness, kindness, self-acceptance, and understanding. If you like, role-play in your mind and imagine yourself being the good and reassuring parent to a frightened child, or imagine someone warm and nurturing from your past talking to you, saying something like, "There, there. You'll get through this. You're doing fine." Repeat that to yourself until you start to feel yourself calming down. (You will.)

By employing these cognitive interventions each time

COACH'S CORNER

As the inhibition of stage two begins to ease, you may still feel fear. But by learning to "live and let live," you'll find that the anxiety doesn't escalate. And each time you succeed at working through stage two, you'll gain confidence that you can do it again. Success builds on success.

stage two of a shyness attack descends upon you, you'll "go with the flow" instead of shutting down or saying more than you planned. And as you add to your personal history of getting through this stage intact, the cumulative effect of these can-do experiences in real-world social situations will slowly enable you to participate in conversations more comfortably. But practice as often as you can to enhance your skills—at cocktail parties and mixers, networking events, even at the gym.

THE "NEW THINK" ON STAGE TWO

To manage stage two, the most important thing to do is perceive your "problem" in a new light to further disarm the fear. Here are several examples of the shifts in thinking that participants in my workshops have made that have helped them to retrieve complete emotional and physical mobility.

- **Remind yourself that others blame themselves.** If you freeze up during a conversation and you're standing with a group, remember that they may not notice. If you're with just one person, she might just as easily think you're reacting to her. Most shyness sufferers expect the world of themselves. In their mistakenly myopic perception, they can't imagine that others can also suffer from pressure to be exemplary. So many of my workshop participants have a heightened sense of perfectionism. But the truth is, Nonshys also feel the pressure to shine when they're on a date or in another social situation, including when they're in bed with someone. Keeping that fact in mind—that everyone feels the pressure to be "on" at times—may help you relax and "help out" by doing some of the work needed to get a conversation flowing.

- **Visualize someone else's weakness.** When you're talking in a group or one-on-one with someone you're interested in, try to imagine what trait might make him afraid, worried, or insecure. Is it his weight, his crooked front teeth, her tendency to lisp, her nervous laugh? In other words, silently do to another person what you do to yourself. Then step back a moment and try to see the person as a whole, as you might have if you hadn't been *trying* to pick him apart. Chances are, this exercise will leave you feeling empathetic for him, and give you a clearer sense of the kindness others may feel toward you.

• **Adopt a self-affirming mantra.** Select one that tells you *how* you want to be. Actively repeating a specific phrase that resonates with you, such as *I'm an interesting person* or *I've got a lot to offer*, can bolster your confidence and override the negative voices you may be hearing. Ted, who was having particular trouble making small talk at singles events, revealed the mantra that worked for him was "Cool, relaxed mind, calm body." He often repeated it throughout this stage of an encounter. "And pretty soon, about ten or fifteen minutes into it, I do feel calm and relaxed," he said. Even though you may feel foolish at first, or not believe what you're telling yourself with your mantra, your mind will be open to suggestion and gradually embrace it.

THE NEXT STEP: ACTION!

Once you get the gist of making cognitive shifts that can help you get into a positive frame of mind, the next step for managing overload is to add behavioral-modification strategies that help you push through the fear. On the following pages are suggestions I frequently propose to my workshop participants to actively manage stage two. By practicing these strategies, you won't necessarily become an extrovert, but in time you may come to intuitively *know* how to ignite a conversation and keep it flowing.

After reading through these ten tactics, rank them in order of difficulty in the space provided, 1 being the easiest you can imagine yourself doing—the activity you're most willing to try—and 10 the most challenging, the biggest stretch for your shyness management skills. Your ranking will be used to enhance your courage score, which we'll rate at the end of this chapter. Before

you go out or on a date, review these exercises. You may be surprised to discover how readily they come to mind and that you
can easily practice them even while conversing, without being
obvious about it. Soon, they will become second nature.

1. **Practice active listening.** Active listening is a technique I
   often recommend to people who have a particularly tough
   time "climbing out of themselves." Ultimately, it forces you
   to clearly hear another person's point of view.

   First, bring yourself into neutral. Think, "I will take a
   deep breath. I will calm myself." If, for example, you tend
   to beat yourself up ("I'm boring" or even just "I'm no good
   at dating"), say to yourself "Stop" or "No." Either of those
   direct orders will often silence a negative pattern of self-talk.
   And remember to breathe. Physical relaxation techniques
   such as soft-belly breathing (breathing into the depths of
   your diaphragm) work best. During a stressful social situation or moment of awkwardness, monitor your breathing by
   inconspicuously placing your hand on your abdomen and
   feeling it rise and fall in sync with each breath.

   Then, to join a conversation, repeat words or phrases the
   speaker used in a question. Piggybacking on spoken words
   with a question is an easy way to keep the conversation
   flowing. For example, if someone says, "I used to live in
   Philadelphia," you might say, "Philadelphia, really? What
   was that like?" Speakers will automatically feel you're interested in them, and the good feeling this generates will
   boost your confidence and enthusiasm.

   Like most things in life, the process of actively listening
   gets better with practice. In fact, trying it out on everyone
   you meet or know can be extremely beneficial. Roberta, an
   investment broker in her mid-thirties, gave it a try during a
   flight from Los Angeles to New York. "I talked to the man
   I was sitting next to for five hours," she said proudly, "a

talkathon." No doubt experiences like that will help Roberta build conversational confidence.

RANK _____

2. **Read between the lines.** Nothing will kill the positive ambiance of a conversation faster than pushing someone to speak about a subject that makes him uncomfortable. It sounds obvious, but it can happen if you take conversational cues from others without filtering and noticing your own feelings in reaction to what you hear. Someone you just met may really want to talk about his divorce or medical procedure or the fact that he's in between jobs and having a hard time making ends meet. But if he moves quickly past the subject, it's a good idea to move on, too. The fact that it was brought up at all may only mean it's on his mind, not that he wants to discuss the issue. Further questions from you could be perceived as intrusive; his general "goodwill" could melt into a sour demeanor, and you could be perilously close to another paralysis or nervous chatter. Another sign that you touched on a taboo subject is when someone avoids answering your question altogether or says something like, "Hard to talk about." Let it pass by offering a transitional remark, such as, "That must be tough. [pause] So, how do you know so-and-so . . . ?"

RANK _____

3. **Have a list of instant icebreakers.** Sometimes, to keep a conversation going, you may be tempted to bring up the first topic that comes to mind, no matter what it is, to fill the gaps that can accompany the initial moments of getting to know someone. The paralysis or gushing you're working through may make it difficult to monitor what you say. So, when you're getting ready for a date, as I discussed earlier, prepare a list of things to talk about, topics

that make others feel comfortable, such as vacations, current events, music, or favorite movies. Some of my clients also make a mental note to avoid talking about illness, money issues, politics, and other relationships. Some tell themselves to avoid lines designed to impress others and insincere-sounding compliments like, "No, really, you have the bluest eyes I've ever seen." Even though you may be trying to be friendly, not everyone you meet may enjoy the flirtatious overtones.

If you do say something that falls flat, so be it. It's generally better not to explain ("What I meant was . . . "); in this case, you will draw attention to what you believe is your spoken misstep. Moving on by changing the subject, even if you perceive the switch to be awkward, will usually provide a smoother recovery.

RANK _____

4. **Briefly talk about yourself.** A good way to get someone talking is to disclose something about yourself that's not too personal but offers a comfortable jumping-off point. (What will your interesting tidbit be? You might want to plan ahead.) Being the first to reveal indicates a willingness for openness. Sensing your generosity, your listener will likely make her own self-disclosure and form a connection with you. Voilà! An instant bond. And once you get rolling, it will be easier for you to speak. If you've just taken a bite of an hors d'oeuvre, you might say, "This is great. I've been taking cooking lessons at the institute for the past few months. Do you like to cook?" Or "I wish I could make this sort of thing. But I'm a klutz in the kitchen. How about you?" The idea is to lob a piece of information about yourself over the net to increase the chances you'll get something in return. Chances are, you will. Conversational generosity is contagious.

RANK _____

5. **Prove you're listening.** People are pleased when there's proof positive you're paying attention to them. Let's face it: Many of us, especially in these frenetic times, nod like crazy while our minds are a zillion miles away. "I heard you mention earlier that . . . " is a way of saying to someone, "I'm paying attention to you." What a compliment—and an effective way to both loosen someone up and put yourself at ease.

RANK _____

6. **Highlight mutual interests.** Letting the listener know you have something in common creates an immediate atmosphere of camaraderie. "It's so great to talk with other people who are into bicycle trips. Nobody realizes how enjoyable it is to travel that way!" Basically, what you're doing is helping your partner feel that you're on the same page, someone who "gets it." You're modeling what you would like to receive from another person—to be joined and appreciated. At some point in the future, it's possible that she will likely return the favor.

RANK _____

7. **React with pleasure.** Even if you have to force it, laugh when it's appropriate. For one thing, it's a way to look more approachable and put others at ease. Smiling or laughing appreciatively will make others feel smart, witty, and eager to be near you. You, in turn, may find yourself regaled with stories to which you can react without feeling pressured to do the entertaining.

RANK _____

8. **Use a little self-effacing humor.** It can't hurt. Trying his luck with a personal matchmaker service in Manhattan,

Matt, a shy single in his forties, was invited to events that reminded him of awkward junior high parties, where the boys stood on one side of the room and the girls on the other. He used that insight about the events to poke fun at himself. "I'm sorry, but I was never good at this sort of thing when I was growing up. And here I am, in middle age, still at the junior high dance. I can almost feel my braces against my teeth. Isn't it funny that we're all here? But I think it's a good thing. . . . "

"I don't use this opening line too often," Matt told the group one evening, "because I'm afraid I'll sound like a broken record. But when I do, I make sure to say it with a smile. The response I almost always get is, 'Gee, I feel that way, too,' or 'Dating really does get harder as we get older, doesn't it?'" Matt was onto something. Overall, laughing at yourself puts others at ease because you seem less perfect. It also gives them a chance to talk about how they feel, which can make you forget about yourself, relax, and enjoy the conversation.

RANK _____

9. **Come back later.** If something's not working, try again later. Pamela, a chef at a popular New York City bistro, was delighted to learn from experience that there's often time to work through stage two by reinitiating contact

COACH'S CORNER

Sometimes the painfully shy think they need to be grateful for any conversation they're in that keeps moving—even if they aren't enjoying their companion. Not true. Yes, you're shy, but you still have the right to decide you'd rather not speak to someone or to end a conversation, even though it may be otherwise rolling along. Politely saying, "Oh, you know, I just saw someone I need to catch before he leaves," or "Actually, I'm getting thirsty. Would you excuse me, please?" are fine options and preserve your right to choose, even if you might worry that the next person you talk to won't be as chatty.

later. "If I can't get my thoughts together when I first meet someone, I excuse myself to get a drink and then I approach him again in fifteen minutes, when I've had time to get used to the room and everything that's going on and think about what I'm going to say," she said. "Or, I talk to someone else for awhile, someone I'm not that interested in, to get my bearings before going up to the man I'd really like to talk to."

RANK _____

10. **Tell it like it is.** Outing yourself also works for stage two. You could say "I'm shy" or, even better, talk about the experiences in which you're shy so you're not completely defined by your shyness. For example, you might say in a positive tone, "Walking into a roomful of strangers is tough

THE BUZZ ABOUT ALCOHOL

Alcohol, or what Indiana University Southeast shyness expert Bernardo Carducci, Ph.D., calls "liquid extroversion," is usually part of the scene at parties and restaurants. If you're dating, chances are you're around it often. Indeed, based on my empirical research, alcohol is the shy person's frequent companion in many uncomfortable situations. Many of my shy singles worry that alcohol might become a crutch.

Of course, anytime you're using alcohol as a form of self-medication, you're in a potentially dangerous situation. Alcohol—for any of us—can become a serious addictive substance if it's used to mask shyness. Alcohol can also rob you of cognitive function, exactly what you don't need when you're trying to manage your shyness. Many of my shy singles who choose to drink impose rules on themselves, such as no more than one or two drinks a night. Their goal is to enjoy themselves without having the alcohol take over. All in all, think of drinking like swimming in the ocean. It can be wonderful, but also perilous. If you don't establish limits, you might get trapped in the undertow.

for me. I can never think of anything to say to people I don't know." By focusing on when you're shy, you can control your image. Avoid negative comments like, "I can't. I'm too shy," or "I could never do that. Crowds are hard for me." Such negative absolutes can be depressing for you and turn off others.

The typical reaction when you tell people you're shy in certain situations is often, "So am I" or "I hate parties, too" or "You don't seem shy." In any event, by revealing your shyness, you begin to clue the other person in to better understanding your reactions. And the more you put feelings into words, the less likely you'll be to act them out. That's a concept that works for everyone—shy and nonshy alike.

RANK _____

YOUR ACTION PLAN

The ten behavioral strategies listed on pages 69–74 involve interfacing with others. Like the five cognitive shifts I outlined on pages 65–68, they'll be part of your strategy for managing dating shyness and increasing your courage one step at a time. To divert overload when you're out socially, employ your number-one-ranked or easiest tactic first. Do it several times until it comes naturally to you, then proceed to your number-two-ranked strategy, and so on. If any action seems too difficult to tackle, you can give yourself half a point on your courage score for just visualizing yourself doing this behavior before an outing. Then, when you're ready, spend as little as five minutes practicing it with other people.

Which strategies will you try? Record your game plan in the space that follows. As I've already mentioned, writing it down makes it real—and more committed to memory. Consider photocopying this page for easy reference when you're in the dating trenches.

I'd like to try to manage my shyness by:

_____

_____

_____

_____

_____

_____

_____

_____

_____

_____

_____

_____

_____

_____

_____

_____

_____

_____

_____

_____

_____

_____

_____

_____

WHAT'S YOUR COURAGE SCORE?

We complete this chapter with your courage score. On a scale of 1 to 10, with 1 being the courage of a kitten (you rarely initiate a conversation at social events; you babble out of control when someone speaks to you) and 10 the courage of a lion (you choose when to speak and rarely freeze or flood), rate your circuit overload courage score. Circle your score below.

1 1.5 2 2.5 3 3.5 4 4.5 5 5.5 6 6.5 7 7.5 8 8.5 9 9.5 10

You may wish to write your score in the space that follows: _____

If your courage score is more kitten than lion—perhaps it's 2—ask yourself what you can incorporate from your action plans to increase your score to a 2.5. For a .5 increase, for example, you might practice piggybacking on someone's conversation by thinking of questions to ask him as you're conversing. Even if you don't actually utter them, that's okay. You're getting in the frame of mind to do so. Since you're now aware of how shy you are in various dating situations—a clearer idea of when the fear of initiation and circuit overload tend to be issues for you as well as an action plan—you have the tools you need to increase your courage score one small increment at a time.

When you experience overload, recalculate your courage score, trying to bring it up another half-point by attempting—or even imagining—one of the cognitive and/or behavioral courage steps suggested in your action plan. Keep in mind that courage means consistently putting one foot in front of the other. As you take on more and more of these exercises, you will see and feel your score gradually improve. Best of all, you'll get the hang of truly being yourself in social situations, and you'll stop associating having a good time with fear.

"The braver a man is, the happier he is."
—*Seneca*, De Tranquillitate Animi, A.D. 60

{FIVE}

THE SHYNESS ATTACK, STAGE THREE: PAYBACK

"I was so nervous on my first date with Gabrielle that I talked *at* her for three hours," said Cole, an advertising agency project manager in his early thirties. "I told her about my new apartment, my new job, where I grew up, and what I like to do on the weekends," he recounted. It sounded reasonable. But in Cole's mind, he had "flooded" big time, and now he was reliving his "rabid" conversational faux pas in Technicolor. "I should have asked her more questions," he said. "I should have excused myself to the restroom and given myself a pep talk. I shouldn't have had two martinis. . . ."

His voice evaporated. Cole was agonizing over the third and final stage of a shyness attack, and the should-haves were consuming him. Perhaps you've been in Cole's shoes. If you've ever mentally played back the previous night or event and nitpicked your social contributions with the linguistic precision of a high school English teacher, you know what it's like to experience payback's anguish.

78

Without question, Cole's sort of experience is one of the most popular topics among the shy singles in my workshops. It's characterized by an obsessive need to replay and critique, in finely detailed terms, the instances of a social event in which you're convinced you made a fool of yourself. Whether you managed to do or say something or stood frozen to the spot, payback occurs when you review your "performance" with the fervor of a movie critic and assail yourself with self-recrimination. In essence, you replay your perceived high-profile or embarrassing moments or interactions, feel as if you could die of embarrassment, and punish yourself for being out there.

ONE FALSE MOVE

As you're working through the stages of a shyness attack, introducing yourself, or conversing with a new dinner companion, you're taking risks and acquiring an account of the event in your mind's eye, both of which can later fuel payback. Any action provides ammunition for this stage of an attack. Consider this: When you construct a fortress to avoid the imagined scrutiny of others—and thus, give in to your shyness—a perfectly legitimate move in the social world, such as introducing a topic of conversation, can seem like it's crossing the line of acceptable behavior. For Shys, less can mean so much more.

The perceived misdeeds that will later inspire payback don't have to be big. It can proliferate from events as small as exchanging glances ('Am I getting a dirty look?') or laughing ('a little too much?') at someone else's attempts at humor. And you don't actually have to command center stage to experience payback later on. The events that subsequently induce it can be as legitimate as answering questions in a conversation or telling a little story about yourself that relates to the context of what's being said. But to your mind—in retrospect, anyway—you were out there in the spotlight for all to scrutinize. And when something actually does happen that draws attention to itself, such as spilling red wine on the hostess's carpet or blanking on someone's name, forget it. Shys magnify the incident out of proportion and hang on, punishing themselves for their "uncoolness," clumsiness, or forgetfulness.

The self-obsessive thinking that characterizes payback can also arise from having done or said nothing, for instance, if you clam up during the hellos (fear of initiation) or fall silent further into a conversation (freezing). Feeling like the odd one out or the only one *not* participating in a conversation can lend itself to the same caliber of self-punishment as having actively—but seemingly incompetently—interacted with others. "I just stood there when everybody else was chattering away," said Monica, a thirty-five-year-old infant wear designer, explaining how she acted at an after-work party. "Somebody I didn't know very well actually said to me, 'Are you feeling okay?' I wanted to crawl under a table." As if freezing weren't difficult enough, Monica couldn't stop from berating herself about her silence for several days. At that party was someone she was trying to impress. "I so blew it," she told the group, grimacing. "If only I could just push the rewind button and do the night over."

If only. A form of self-punishment, payback is what I consider to be the cruelest stage of a shyness attack because you give yourself no credit for *trying*, even for just being present, which indeed deserves credit. Maybe you know it well. Here's a sampling of the payback-inspired comments I've heard:

"How could I have been so stupid (or insensitive, boring, aggressive)?"

"That person will never want to talk (or dance, sit, study, debate, sleep) with me again."

"I'm incompetent (or a jerk, a loser, a low-life)."

"If only I had said it with a smile (or a frown, humor, sarcasm)."

"I felt so dumb (lost, inadequate, juvenile) just standing there."

"How could I have said (done, touched, laughed at, revealed, asserted, denounced, approved, acknowledged) that?"

YOUR OWN WORST ENEMY

Karen, a forty-two-year-old nurse, is just one of my clients who was a pro at payback, said, "If I have a date on a Friday night, I'll sit on my couch the rest of the weekend and stew over everything I said and did. I just can't help it." Others in the group nodded. During this stage of an attack, Shys seem compelled to pay themselves back for the "audacity" of venturing out and acting as if they're not shy.

Typically, payback occurs after you've been in a dating or other social situation in which you were uncomfortable and couldn't find your bearings. Stage one and/or stage two may be its source. For example, if you stutter your name during an introduction (stage one), you may feel sick at the recollection when you're home from the party recounting the night. Or, if you believe you said too much or too little during the evening (stage two), payback may pay you a call.

The essence of payback is torturous self-review about what you consider to be your worst social moments at a particular event, relived the next day, and perhaps for days afterward. "The goodnight kiss is always what does it for me," said Terri, a single mother in her late thirties, cringing. "When I see the kiss coming, I get nervous and start moving. It happened again when I was on a date with

COACH'S CORNER

If you're an expert at payback, you probably have the tendency to unrealistically compare yourself to the most socially outgoing person in the room. But next time you're at a party, look around. You'll probably notice that, just like you, many others are listeners, rather than the so-called life of the party.

someone brand new. We ended up bobbing heads. I was so embarrassed! I re-experienced that botched kiss for a week. I can't believe I'm almost forty and I don't even know how to kiss, or at least, I don't look like I do," she said.

THE ROOTS OF PAYBACK

Like the other two stages of a shyness attack, payback may be influenced by your personal history. We all harbor voices from our pasts that color our experiences, our behavior, and our perceptions of others. These voices usually originate from messages we received from childhood authority figures such as parents, relatives, teachers, or older siblings. If the exchanges (spoken or implied) were mostly positive—such as "You can do anything you put your mind to"—they can generate encouraging self-talk (rather than payback) in adulthood that can build confidence, and in the workplace, enhance productivity. But if the childhood messages were more often negative—such as "Don't talk back!" "Don't contradict me," "You'll never amount to much," or even "What's the matter with you? You're useless"—the adult may be afraid to take an assertive position, stick up for himself, make decisions, do something new, or take charge of his life, especially during vulnerable periods of social pressure, like at a party or on a date.

To break free from this negative self-image, the key is to gain awareness of how it developed in your life. For everyone, digging deeply is the first step. I like the simple methods of Muriel James, Ed.D., author of *It's Never Too Late to Be Happy*. She suggests that once you understand where your self-talk originates, you can develop strategies to replace it with positive, loving talk. "If you had an overly critical father, for example, and you realize you become extremely self-critical when you're under pressure (and afterwards), imagine a parent who has the opposite of your father's qualities," says James. Start by talking back and creating a mantra such as, "I'm competent and I've done well at this before. I can do it again." You can even use humor if you like, such as "I'm funny. I'm smart. And I make a mean chocolate chip cookie. Who wouldn't want me?"

As you're getting the hang of that approach, take it a step further and try to learn to be as understanding with yourself as you would be with a child. Start by thinking of a nurturing adult from your past—or present—and put kind words into her mouth. In general, what you choose to say to yourself should reflect what an ideal, affirming parent or encouraging authority figure would say so that you, in effect, comfort yourself when dealing with payback. If your child came home crying because she was too afraid to give her speech in front of the class, would you tell her she's a big loser? Or would you say, "Keep trying. Many people are afraid to talk in front of others. And remember, you're good at lots of other things." That's the idea.

Frequently, impossibly high expectations are at the root of many payback attacks. "It's almost like I don't allow myself to be human," said Irene, a forty-six-year-old mother of two teenagers who started dating again after twenty years. Irene often experienced it after first dates because "I have no idea what I'm doing," she confessed. When a person experiences payback, she masks uncomfortable emotions such as feeling ill at ease or self-conscious with rambling, self-critical thoughts. There's no resolve or hope for the future, only negativity and despair.

THE FUNCTIONS OF PAYBACK

This anxiety serves several functions, which is why it is so compelling and can be as tough to shake as a bad cold. For one, it's a protective preemptive strike. In your mind, you may believe it stands between you and the voices of others who might insult you or criticize your every move—unless, of course, you get there first. In a less-conscious manner, you are attempting to control what you cannot control, such as other people's opinions expressed behind your back. I know it's not rational, but most of us are often ruled by emotions over intellect. And as uncomfortable as it is to be punished with obsessive thoughts about your own perceived failings, it's emotionally safer to hear them from yourself than from someone else—which is what you imagine is already happening anyway. For example, 'I can't believe I actually wore a Hawaiian shirt and sandals to a winter "luau." Everyone else knew that theme just reflected the party's menu and not the dress code. How could I have been so stupid?'

Payback is also a sign that you felt you were "out of your element." Like a near-miss auto accident, you brushed up against danger, and you can't help but flash back to it. Flashbacks are reflexive mental reactions meant for self-protection; i.e., 'If I go over this again and again, maybe I can learn something that will prevent a future accident/social misstep.' Discomfort with being center stage in a play for which you have no script can trigger a mental filibuster when you take a stand of any kind. "How could I have done that? What was I thinking?" are common questions that spark the payback debate. These are disingenuous questions because they aren't what you really want to know. The real question is: "Do I have a right to speak up?" In my experience, many shy singles aren't sure of that answer, so they attack themselves. They don't really believe they played that unfamiliar role very well—whether it's being a guest at a chi-chi party, hosting a dinner, or being the other person on a date.

Payback becomes less of an issue—even a nonissue—when you clearly understand the boundaries of a role you're in, a role that seems natural to you because you have full use of your personal faculties. "I never go through payback after I give a speech to a conference room full of strangers," said Marsha, a perplexed executive recruiter. She's puzzled because in the business role, she doesn't feel vulnerable. "But when I'm at the receptions that follow the speeches and trying to circulate, I monitor my every syllable and stumble over my words. Sometimes even I can't believe I'm the same person who just wowed the crowd," she said.

For those who are confident and secure in other areas of their lives, dating can be tortuous. Eileen, an associate television producer in her late twenties, had no problem with payback after business events, such as the company's corporate picnic. "I feel completely comfortable when I can talk shop," she said. "If only I could do that on dates with men who aren't in my industry," she concluded. Indeed, when the role you're in isn't a cushy fit—like being on a first, second, or even third date (with someone who, for example, isn't in your line of work); hanging out at a bar trying to look relaxed; or revealing yourself online—your insecurity can cause you to intensely monitor your every action and reaction, all to be played back again and again later.

Tidal waves of guilt and shame underlie this form of obsessive thinking; payback masks these undercurrents. Guilt occurs when we feel as if we have violated a role boundary—like feeling guilty about taking two pieces of pie and leaving none for the other person. Shame is feeling that something about us that we can't change is unacceptable, such as the color of our skin, our family's religion, or our mother's accent. Shys may see themselves as inferior when they socialize or are with people who are important to them. Typically, they admonish themselves for saying or doing something unacceptable—like wearing the wrong outfit; trying to enter a conversation (later castigating themselves for having been invasive, aggres-

COACH'S CORNER

Payback isn't exclusive to socializing. You may experience it in relation to other roles in your life, too, ones in which you don't feel secure. If that's the case, many of the management strategies at the end of this chapter will apply.

sive, or inappropriate); or smelling of garlic or not being sexually ready in an intimate situation—when, in fact, they were probably perfectly appealing on all counts. Yet they feel they don't measure up. Their shame triggers guilt for stepping "out of bounds" or acting "inappropriately."

The obsessive thinking that characterizes payback is actually an uncontrolled, repetitive response that falls within a wider family of addictive behaviors, like drug or alcohol abuse; these behaviors are a poorly directed attempt to self-soothe when a person has a low tolerance for frustration or imperfection. But ironically, we layer another negative experience (the payback) over the original stressor (the low tolerance for frustration). Payback perpetuates negativity. Moreover, the more you participate, the deeper and more tangled your thoughts can become. Payback isn't unlike other addictions. The more you indulge, the greater your need, but you never will feel satisfied. It's a vicious cycle.

A DEFENSE MECHANISM THAT ISOLATES

Be aware that payback can also harbor a sneaky opposite reaction that can foster the same isolating result as negative self-talk: that is, feeling superior. Instead of beating yourself up after a date or other event, you obsess over how much better you are than everyone else and wonder where in the world you'll ever fit in. Of course, many people worry about finding the right match, someone who is "good enough" and who offers that special something that feels comfortable and familiar. But superiority is different. It's often a reaction to a buried feeling of inadequacy. You're in arrogant mode when you have thoughts like 'I'll never find someone who's as smart/articulate/sensitive as I am,' which can magnify a sense of hopelessness—not productive in these challenging dating times. If you've ever had an experience like this, you recognize how grandiosity, like obsessive self-criticism, can make you turn inward when you're out socializing and mentally distance yourself from others.

Caroline, the shy single I mentioned in chapter one who couldn't muster up the courage to date at all, was particularly adept at feeling above others. It came on in full force one night when she decided to try her hand at the bar scene with two nonshy women from her office. (Actually, the women had corralled Caroline into going out when she couldn't think of an excuse fast enough to bow out.) Caroline soon found herself sitting at a bar, trying to look relaxed. "My friends quickly started talking with three men, and there I was listening to them. At first, I wanted to join in, but then I was so bored and annoyed by what they were talking about, which was so immature—like what they liked to watch on cable," she sniffed.

In time, Caroline saw her sense of superiority for what it actually was: a cover-up for the fear and insecurity she truly felt. "I never realized I was terrified because I believed no one would ever truly value or welcome me," she said. Putting herself on a pedestal during a dicey dating situation was her way of coping. "To snap out of it, I started to say to myself during a date, 'Okay, Caroline, you're uncomfortable. Take a breath and be yourself.' Just being more real and normal keeps my nose out of the ozone layer."

Another trick you might try: Remind yourself that you can learn something from everyone you encounter; even small children, for example, have their own wisdom. So when you feel a "superiority" attack coming on, tell yourself that you could be missing out on whatever slice of life information that person might have to offer.

PAYBACK'S PENALTIES

What makes payback particularly damaging is that it can lead Shys to avoid the people, places, or situations in which they feel they were vulnerable or in which they believe the world saw them at their worst and can't forget about it. And let's face it: If you're anxious and under pressure in social situations, embarrassing things can happen. One of my shy singles, Lydia, told a story of the time she was the maid of honor at a good friend's wedding and accidentally winked at the best man, who had just told her he had a girlfriend with whom he was serious. "I wasn't at all interested in him," she said. "It just happened out of nervousness because he and I had to stand facing each other during the ceremony in front of the entire congregation right by the bride and groom, apart from the other members of the wedding party. I couldn't handle suddenly being the center of attention like that and for some reason, I winked. It was totally out of character. And, of course, the best man gave me a weird look." Never mind the lovely wedding Lydia had participated in—she played back the moment of the wink for weeks afterwards. Although Lydia can now laugh about the experience (it was six years ago), she's in no hurry to face the best man. "Thank God he lives in San Francisco and I live in New York," she said.

Indeed, avoidance can last a long time. In Lydia's case, if she never sees the best man she winked at again, so be it. But if the person or situation you're paying yourself back for lives right in your neighborhood or regularly appears in the course of your day, you can end up severely limiting where you go. And, of course, the constant sidestepping can be tiresome and inconvenient. Many of my clients admit that payback prevents them from attending social situations altogether because they dread the aftermath.

Stage three can further erode

COACH'S CORNER

If you react to a self-diagnosed blunder by staying home for a while afterward, minimize the aftermath of payback by patting yourself on the back for enjoying your own company. Your "slips" don't have to become falls.

your self-esteem and your confidence. That's because unlike in the first two stages of a shyness attack, the events that provoke payback are over and done with. The first two stages are on-the-spot reactions to what's happening around you. The possibility of change, the sense that you can alter your course if you need to, exists (which offers its own tensions and responsibilities, to be sure). Nonetheless, by the time payback comes around, it's a done deal. You have nowhere to go but inward.

In one of my workshops, Joel, a twenty-seven-year-old marketing executive, said, "Payback hits me the most after I've been to a high-stakes event, like a second date in which I think I might really like the woman. After that, I torture myself for days. I can be so brutal on myself. Sometimes I even wonder if it's worth going out at all." But then, Amy, a fifth-grade teacher, reminded Joel that sitting home night after night wasn't healthy either. The only thing guaranteed to happen by staying home was nothing.

COACH'S CORNER

When reflecting on a conversational moment when you couldn't think of something to say, be kind to yourself. Your compassionate inner dialogue could sound like this: *I felt so uncomfortable. I wish I'd been able to talk. But I'm shy, so it makes it difficult for me to chat when I hardly know anyone!* Likewise, if you have the general sense you made a fool of yourself at a party but have no specific reason to think so, shake your head with compassion and declare, *Look, I always feel this way. It's because I'm shy and afraid everything I do is wrong. Chances are, I was fine.* Cutting yourself slack takes practice, but in time, it gets easier, and it's important. Empathy is the road to self-acceptance.

Converting Payback to Pay Dirt

Take heart, because there is a solution. After you understand from where your payback emanates, you need to learn how to anticipate and tolerate its discomforts. Like the other stages of a shyness attack, stage three runs in predictable patterns. For example, do you always experience it after first and second dates, but not after third and fourth dates? Or does it emerge as you get to know someone? (This may be the case if you're shy around people you know rather than those you don't know.)

To help you determine how you experience payback, take a moment now to assess when this unproductive stage affects you most. Write down three situations in which you played back the events of a date or social event and obsessively criticized your "performance."

Payback often overcomes me when:

1. _____

_____

_____

_____

_____

_____

2. _____

_____

_____

_____

_____

_____

3. _____

_____

_____

_____

_____

_____

Based on what you've written on page 90, what's your verdict? Do you note any similarities among your payback experiences? If so, write your thoughts below by completing the statement, *Payback often overcomes me when:*

———————————————————————————————

———————————————————————————————

———————————————————————————————

———————————————————————————————

———————————————————————————————

———————————————————————————————

To minimize the actual time spent nitpicking the previous night's behavior, try to see the half-full version of the water glass. In thinking about each of the situations you listed on page 90, give yourself credit for taking the risk to expand and grow. That practice is fundamental to thwarting stage three. And keep in mind that none of us can guarantee that we won't offend someone when we're out socially or avoid feeling offended. All spontaneous living is trial and error.

Once you recognize the subtleties of payback, you'll understand yourself better, and this stage will gradually lose its hold over you. In fact, that's true for all three stages of a shyness attack, but especially with this one. You'll know you've succeeded when you have less desire to obsess over what you said or did post-date or post-event. It doesn't mean you're perfect or that you may not occasionally make a faux pas—like we all do at times. It means that you can accept your perceived social imperfections and move on.

DOABLE DEEDS TO MANAGE STAGE THREE

Of course, there's more to managing payback than just giving yourself credit for going out there. On pages 92–99 are ten tips that can help to lessen its painful hold. Rank them in order of difficulty in the space provided, 1 being the easiest solution you can imagine yourself doing, 10 the most challenging. This ranking will be used to enhance your courage score, which we'll discuss at the end of this chapter.

1. **Name it.** Like circuit overload, one of the most effective interventions to stop payback is to name it while it's happening. As soon as you've recognized that you've pushed the rewind button in your mind and have begun to beat yourself up for all you said and did at a social event (or didn't say or do), label it. This can range from saying something to yourself like, "Oh, I feel a payback moment coming on," or "Here I am again, obsessing over everything I said and did," to "I was so boring. Oops—this is payback," or even "I was too intellectual for them. Wait. I could be covering up for my insecurities." The sooner you call it what it is, the more possibility you have to distance yourself from your shame-inducing, negative thoughts.

   RANK _____

2. **Assess rather than obsess.** To reduce the urge to indulge, remind yourself that by obsessing, you're avoiding a realistic self-review—the process of *assessing* exactly why things, in retrospect, didn't go the way you would have liked. With realistic self-review, negative thoughts are transformed into constructive self-awareness that's a springboard for improvement. In this case, you don't make yourself solely responsible for an interaction's downfall—if, in fact, there was one. You accept that there's room for self-improvement—then move on.

   RANK _____

3. **Give yourself permission to obsess . . . less and less.** It may sound counterintuitive, but another helpful technique is to wallow for a fixed period, then start to decrease the time allowed. For example, the next time payback occurs, check the clock and allow yourself an hour to berate yourself. A finite time frame, like during your morning commute, works best. During your obsessive sixty minutes, don't censor your thoughts. Let them flow, even if they're brutal. But when the hour is up, tell yourself that that's it for now; you can do it again tomorrow. The next day, do the same thing: Check the clock, but this time, give yourself only forty-five minutes for self-critical thoughts. Each time you obsess, you may find that you *want* to less. What seemed so important at first will eventually lose its power. By practicing disciplined payback, you'll objectify what you're doing and allow yourself to hold on to this defense for as long as you need it, which will naturally decrease payback's intensity.

   RANK _____

4. **Procrastinate.** If you find yourself in payback at an inconvenient time, such as when you're going to be with others or at work, promise yourself to do it later. 'Wait until I get home and have a bath,' you might negotiate with yourself. Or 'Save this for later.' Silently torturing yourself when you're with others isn't fair to them and can detract from a positive social experience. But knowing you can return to the scene of the crime, so to speak, will help you put it aside for a while—and obsess later if you still need to.

   RANK _____

5. **Make an appointment.** If you're so worried about a social experience that you can't shake the urge to dwell on it, try

PAYBACK VS. REALISTIC SELF-REVIEW

While payback is fueled by insecurity and fear, *realistic* self-review stems from the desire to put your best foot forward, despite your shyness. Its premise is self-acceptance. The creative review progresses from an idea, to ruminating about it, to a new resolution. Conversely, with obsessive thinking, the system is closed to self-forgiveness, personal growth, and hope for the future. You go from "I can't believe I said that" to "I always stick my foot in my mouth" and back again. No matter where your thoughts travel, you return to the same repetitive judgments. To help you tell the difference, here's an example of obsessive and self-critical thoughts contrasted with empowering self-review:

Obsessive critical thought: "I think I probably bored everyone. I kept going on and on about my trip. I'm sure I bored everyone. Their eyes were glazing over when I was speaking."

Realistic self-review: "I think I probably bored everyone because I kept going on and on about my trip. But they did keep asking me questions about it, so maybe they weren't all that bored. But there was that woman with the blue dress who kept shifting her weight. Oh, well. I was excited about my vacation. But next time, I think I'm just going to talk about my trip briefly and ask others questions to give them a chance to talk. And besides, you can't please everyone."

Managing payback also means learning to differentiate between social gaffes and the normal, appropriate give-and-take of

this: Make a commitment to obsess for as many hours as you can manage in one shot, then gradually cut yourself off. It's like deciding to try to lose weight by allowing yourself to eat anything you want. Gradually, the forbidden foods you crave may lose their allure. So it goes with payback.

One workshop participant, Alan, a successful businessman who had just started dating someone he really a conversation. In fact, once you get payback under control, you may not even reconsider the things for which you previously criticized yourself. Rick, a shy single in his mid-forties, said, "Now when I get home after a date, I still review what happened, but I focus less on myself and everything I said and did. Instead, I concentrate on how we interacted as a couple and how I felt about her. I use that information to decide if I want another date." Rick has transformed obsessive negative thinking into realistic self-review. This provides conclusions on which he can base his future dating plans.

Overall, your goal is to recognize when something may have gone wrong and whether you were to blame or, maybe, that it was all in your head. The ability to give yourself the benefit of the doubt is a difficult skill to master, but it's worth the effort, as Wendy, a workshop participant, can attest. "If I'd been more talkative at the dinner, everyone around me would not have been bored. I was a drag and brought everyone down," she told the group one evening. A groan spread throughout the room. "Oh, there I go again, thinking obsessively," Wendy said, immediately recognizing her error, then correcting herself. "But why should I make myself responsible for the dinner conversation? It wasn't up to me to carry the whole thing. I was a guest, not the hostess, and even so . . . " Her voice trailed off as she started to look doubtful again. But she was on the right track. "That's the spirit," someone shouted out, for support. And indeed, it was.

liked, tried this strategy during an eleven-hour flight to Asia. In his case, the woman he was dating was "lovely, smart, witty, and capable." All terrific qualities, of course. But not necessarily for Alan. "I'm in over my head," he decided. And after every date, he'd obsess over where he'd failed or could have done better. Alan decided to use his business trip as an experiment. He made a commitment to obsess for as many hours as he could manage while in flight. Whatever that number was, the next day he agreed to criticize for an equal number of hours minus one, and so forth. He followed that pattern each successive day of his trip. If this mentally exhaustive strategy didn't work and he felt he needed to think more, we agreed he would

WHEN YOU FEEL THE NEED TO SMOOTH THINGS OVER

Occasionally, there could be a situation in which you actually say or do something inappropriate to someone; acknowledge this, and apologize for what you said or did. Things happen. That's part of the healing process: to be able to face a mistake, recognizing how and why it occurred, taking responsibility for it, and still thinking the whole thing mostly went well and that you're okay. And remember, few social blunders are actually as bad as you think they are.

If, after you've gained some distance and perspective about the incidents that inspired your replay episode, you still think you might have offended someone, I suggest practicing what you'd like to say to avoid spurring on even more payback; you might even write yourself a script. For example, "I felt bad the other afternoon. The comment I made about your hair came out all wrong. I hope I didn't sound rude." Because of shyness, you may say these things without much gusto or conviction, self-consciously looking away or speaking softly. But that's okay. In truth, you're revisiting this issue largely so you can feel better about you. (In which case, simply saying your piece aloud to yourself may be enough to relieve your anguish.)

Many of my workshop participants tell me how surprised they are to learn that the other people they "insulted" weren't offended at all—or if they were, they were over it. "Jim didn't even know what I was talking about," said Randi, who worried for days about her off-the-cuff comment about the jacket Jim was wearing on their first date; it was worsted wool—in the summer. Okay, so Jim could use a little fashion advice. Nonetheless, "I was so relieved that he wasn't mad," Randi said.

next try adding an hour to his payback "schedule." By the time Alan returned from Asia, he had called a halt to this "game." "I've hardly obsessed since, and I'm much more comfortable with myself in this relationship," he told me. (After several days, Alan managed to turn many of his obsessive thoughts into realistic self-review.) "Maybe I'm not so out of my league," he said.

The downside to this tactic is that it can be time consuming (it can take several days to exhaust excessive thoughts). Still, many Shys find it reassuring to know it's an option, especially if they have a block of time, like a flight or a layover, where they have a finite amount of time as a boundary.

RANK _____

6. **Give yourself the benefit of the doubt.** Although time to detach can help clarify issues that induce payback, if you can't separate yourself from the emotions of the experience it can also distort reality. For example, 'Maybe when I said that about Tim's taste in furniture, I hurt his feelings' can rapidly become 'I can't believe how insensitive and stupid I can be.' An hour later you might be up to 'Tim will probably never call, even though he said he would. He probably hates me. And why shouldn't he?' And so forth. A better idea: If you think you blundered, try sidelining any self-critical litany. For example, you could say to yourself, 'It's possible I didn't sound as insulting as

COACH'S CORNER

When you do or say something you consider to be impulsive or out of character, you may immediately imagine you've blundered. Maybe you have, maybe you haven't; it makes no difference. To combat this fumbling feeling, remind yourself that your characteristic style of repeating your personal patterns ad nauseam (i.e., payback) can also make you feel just that . . . emotionally nauseous.

I thought I did. After all, his furniture was unusual. I'll think it through again, say, tomorrow morning.' Taking a step back may mellow your interpretations and help you accept that what you said probably bothered you more than it did the other person.

RANK _____

7. **Exercise your cares away.** There's nothing like working out to help you break a negative train of thought and burn off steam. Exercise in general is beneficial for stress relief. Choose an activity that demands your undivided attention. Team sports, dance classes, or challenging mountain biking work well. So does a walking meditation, where you concentrate on feeling your feet touch the ground with each step and silently repeat a soothing phrase such as "easy does it." Mind/body awareness can help focus your mind in the present. Without a mantra, you're apt to exercise *and* worry and deprive yourself of that much-needed mental break. A hobby, such as studying a new language or taking up a musical instrument, can also take your mind off belittling thoughts.

RANK _____

8. **Transform obsessive, self-annihilating thoughts.** If, upon reflection, you feel you really were insensitive or rude or silly, accept it, feel bad, conclude you'll be more careful next time, and move on. Although that may be easier said than done, one of the most effective ways for turning payback into insight is to ask yourself: *What did I learn from that experience?* When you study your behavior subjectively, you'll become more aware of "how to be" when you're in a similar situation. Chances are, things will go more to your liking.

RANK _____

9. **Remember, nobody's perfect.** Appreciate your imperfections. After all, they make you exciting, vulnerable, and approachable! In general, faux pas make us human—and interesting. If we were all socially flawless, we'd be robots.

RANK _____

10. **Repeat a mantra.** For Shys, self-acceptance can be as tough to incorporate as egg yolks into a saucepan of hot cream. That's why I often suggest my clients learn a saying, which I've dubbed the Paybacker's Creed:

I'm shy. I'm human. I make mistakes. But they don't define who I am. Some mistakes are real. Some I just imagine. But I don't deserve to be punished for them. I need to learn from them, and I deserve to forgive myself and move forward.

When you feel an attack coming on, remind yourself of this mantra. Repeat it with each episode you encounter. You might even consider printing it and placing it where you can see it often. It can help you reprogram your thinking and overpower the negative thoughts that spawn this debilitating stage.

YOUR ACTION PLAN

The ten strategies listed on pages 92–99 focus on increasing your courage, one step at a time. After you've ranked them, pick one you think might help to diminish your payback cycle; begin by trying your easiest strategy. If even this seems too difficult to tackle, you can give yourself half a point on your courage score for just visualizing yourself doing it. When you're ready, spend as little as five minutes practicing it. If your payback doesn't lessen, try another strategy and keep trying until one, or some combination, of these strategies does the trick.

Which strategies will you try? Record your game plan in the space on page 100. Consider photocopying your plan for easy reference when you return from an evening in the dating trenches.

I'd like to try to manage my payback by:

WHAT'S YOUR COURAGE SCORE?

We complete this chapter with your courage score. On a scale of 1 to 10, with 1 being the courage of a kitten (you frequently call yourself on nearly everything you say and do), and 10 the courage of a lion (after a dating event, you assess the situation by thinking mostly about what went right), rate your payback courage score. Circle your score below.

1 1.5 **2** 2.5 **3** 3.5 **4** 4.5 **5** 5.5 **6** 6.5 **7** 7.5 **8** 8.5 **9** 9.5 **10**

You may wish to write your score in the space that follows: _____

If your courage score is more kitten than lion—perhaps it's 2.5—ask yourself what you can incorporate from your action plans to increase your score to 3. A .5 increase, for example, might involve focusing—even for just five minutes a day—on what you learned from experiences that inspired payback over the course of the next week. That can help you shift your thinking in the right direction.

When you experience a carping self-review, recalculate your courage score, trying to bring it up another half point by attempting—or even imagining—one of the courage-building steps in your action plan. Remember, courage is consistently putting one foot in front of the other, with each small, measured step soon adding up to increasing empowerment. It takes step-by-step effort to give up the familiar defense of payback.

"To dare is to lose one's footing momentarily.
To not dare is to lose oneself."

—Søren Kierkegaard

{SIX}

SEVEN HABITS OF THE SOCIALLY FIT

NEW YORK CITY can be one of the toughest places in the world to live and work—and date—especially if you're shy. The city is competitive. Bustling. Hectic. Confusing. And potentially isolating. "Even though there are millions of people, you can still feel alone. You have to work at finding your niche," said Kevin, a shy single in his early forties. In my shyness workshops, many others often echo Kevin's sentiments. To its credit, the city provides a level of anonymity that can be refreshingly freeing at first, especially if a person grew up in a small, claustrophobic town. But, in time, it can emotionally isolate the shy. Sure, you can sing an aria on the street corner if you want to and nobody will pay you any mind. You can eat in the world's finest restaurants and rub shoulders with the famous. "But something as simple as dating regularly, or finding someone 'normal' or approachable can seem impossible," said Melinda, another shy client. "Dating in New York can be scary." No doubt, where you live and work also has its own unique set of dating challenges.

Although the shy comprise a sizable percentage of my practice, I also regularly meet with nonshy clients who come to me for myriad other reasons. And while it may be true that New York City is a challenging place to meet someone and get to know them, I've noticed that many of these nonshy folks do just fine. It's not that their dating lives are perfect—certainly, they have their share of horror stories. Yet, they steadily meet new people in what could be perceived as a treacherous dating zone. It often occurs to me that my shy clients could benefit by taking a page from their books. After all, the repetitive strategies extroverts use to find a good match, develop a social network, keep themselves in circulation, and, if they're lucky, have a great romance aren't theirs exclusively.

In fact, research conducted by shyness expert Philip Zimbardo, Ph.D., and others supports the possibility that anyone can develop the tools of the socially savvy, even if they're genetically hardwired for shyness, although they may need to slightly modify the methods. Even the nonshy aren't immune; sometimes they also have to cultivate and nurture these habits. The secret is to try various techniques, like those I outline in this chapter and throughout the book, again and again.

This practice-makes-perfect concept is part of a new trend called social fitness, a term first used in relation to shyness at the Shyness Institute. The theory holds that if you're shy or socially anxious, you're simply "out of shape" emotionally. Through regular "workouts," you may be able to tone and strengthen your behavior, thinking patterns, and attitudes and become more skilled at regulating your emotions. While social fitness doesn't change who you are—it won't, for example, make you unshy—it will help you better deal with the emotions that govern this trait. Social fitness isn't unlike training for a decathlon by working out regularly. Many of my shy clients feel their emotional skills improving as they put themselves through the dating paces, similar to the exuberant feeling of no longer being winded after a good run. By going out there and practicing your shyness management skills, you can develop more dating "muscle."

GETTING YOURSELF IN DATING SHAPE

But what does it take to become more socially buff? What approaches do Nonshys try that you can mimic? To answer that question, I informally polled a large group of my nonshy clients for their best dating strategies. Consider them your emotional fitness trainers. Following are seven habits they've honed that work for them again and again. Some of these strategies take guts. Some of them you may never attempt. Still, if you modify them slightly—making them more comfortable and more doable for you—they're worth a try.

Habit #1: Hang Out with the Opposite Sex

If you can manage the initial discomfort, it's worth joining an established group in which most members are of the gender you're seeking. Shy men who want to meet women might consider taking a course like flower arranging, pottery, or home decorating (ideally, whatever you sign up for should truly interest you) or joining a reading group at the library or local bookstore. Dance, yoga, or Pilates classes are also excellent options for men. Women who want to meet men might consider enrolling in home improvement, landscaping, or architecture classes, or frequenting places where men get together. "I go to the upscale sports bar in my neighborhood and have dinner with a friend whenever there's a play-off or season finale," said Sharon, a nonshy single in her mid-thirties who works in the information technology industry. "Then, we go to the bar for one drink. It's a great way to meet sports-minded men who aren't really drinkers, which is a criterion of mine. When it's a really big game, men come in throngs to watch. I haven't met anybody yet, but I know I will," she said confidently.

Barbara, a nonshy divorced mother of three, plays pool to

meet men. She joined a league in her neighborhood in which four players are matched together weekly. "Most of the people I've met through my pool league are men, and I love it," she gushed, setting her sights on one man in particular. Aidan, another Nonshy, said he has had his best luck meeting women by attending Weight Watchers meetings. "I was trying to lose a few pounds, and I also met several women to date," he confided.

You're probably thinking, 'That's fine for them, but not me. Yikes!' The reality is it takes courage to join in a social situation that predominantly features members of the opposite sex. In fact, according to a survey published in *Psychology Today*, conducted by Bernardo Carducci, Ph.D., director of the Shyness Research Institute at Indiana University Southeast, being the only woman in a group of men or vice versa is the second most common shyness-inducing experience, after being with strangers.

Still, you can modify this socially confident strategy. If it's too scary to go alone, you might try bringing a buddy to mixed-gender events. If your buddy agrees to this role, you may feel more comfortable. A shy client of mine, Ramona, attends organized singles' events with an extroverted male friend with whom she's not romantically interested. "If I see someone I think I might like, I'll signal to my friend to start talking with him. Then I'll come up and my friend will introduce me." This strategy can work both ways, especially if your buddy of the opposite sex happens to be shy around those he doesn't know. If he sees someone he's interested in, you can pave the way by talking to the woman first, then introduce him to her when he ambles over. To give yourself a confidence boost, cultivating a sense of altruism can help. "Before going up to a group of guys I don't know, I tell myself, 'Remember, I'm doing this for Olivia,'" said Ted, a shy single in his mid-twenties.

The buddy system, in general, is an effective dating strategy for shy singles, given a few caveats (which you may wish to spell out if you suspect your buddy doesn't "get it"). Your buddy's role is to facilitate the dialogue without taking over. She needs to stay with you (unless you feel comfortable), even if something or someone more exciting comes along, lest you find yourself precariously stranded.

The best buddies also compliment your traits. If you're shy around strangers, you'll probably fare best with a buddy who's extroverted. "I wasn't doing too well with dating until my best friend, Kate, came to New York City from the Midwest," confessed Tori, a former Midwesterner herself. "Kate had always been extremely outgoing. She wanted to check out the New York social scene after separating from her husband. But she needed someone to go out with and luckily that was me because through Kate, I met my husband." Kate met Richard at a restaurant opening and then introduced him to Tori. They quickly discovered they both liked to jog, agreed to meet on the weekend for brunch, and voilà, three years later they were married.

You never know what the buddy system may yield—if you choose the right one. Being a shy person's companion at a social event is a responsibility. After all, there's nothing worse than thinking you're with someone who's up for the job, then ditches you during the event. "When that happened to me last month at a party—my buddy started dancing with someone as soon as the music started—I just left," said Yvonne, a shy single in her late twenties. "And I haven't gone out since."

COACH'S CORNER

Extroverted buddies benefit greatly from having a shy friend—so if you feel like a social parasite, don't. It's a misplaced emotion. As the shy friend, you enhance your pal's confidence and reinforce her courage just by being with her. After all, nobody likes to be alone at certain events—not even extroverts.

Another excellent option for increasing your contacts is to join a group of people with a common aim or interest. They can be fertile places to meet others because they're structured, and often the same people attend regular meetings. By showing up consistently, you increase the chances that someone will greet you or that you'll feel comfortable enough to greet others. Consider, for example, the following options; there are plenty more out there:

- Take a Dale Carnegie course (www.dale-carnegie.com). These courses aim to improve interpersonal and business communication skills and generally attract men and women alike. Even if you don't meet someone, you're bound to get some take-home benefits you can use in your daily life.

- Toastmasters International (www.toastmasters.org) is an excellent way to meet others and hone your public speaking skills. And you usually don't have to speak or participate in any way until you feel comfortable.

- The Sierra Club has chapters for like-minded environmentalists around the country; visit www.sierraclub.org to find one in your area.

- The Volkssports Association is a great venue for meeting others who are into walking as a sport. Log on to www.ava.org for a national network of 350 walking clubs. There's bound to be one in your area.

- The Amateur Rowing Association (www.ara-rowing.org) is an adventurous option if you live near water. Or, if you like hiking or backpacking, try www.hikingandbackpacking.com to find a club near you.

- Consider reconnecting with the local chapter of your old college sorority or fraternity (most people know at least one other person who is single).

- Join a professional organization that's related to your work. But don't be anonymous; get on a committee. It's a way to expand your social circle to include people with whom you automatically have something in common.

- And there's always your church or synagogue. Does it hold any events for singles or sponsor events in which a variety of people are apt to attend, such as fund-raisers?

Volunteering with an organization that interests you is another great way to meet others and boost your social fitness. Focusing the limelight on the goals of the organization and/or the lives of others may reduce your self-consciousness. An added bonus: Besides meeting others who share a common goal, studies show that the altruism you feel by being actively involved with a charitable organization may boost your immune system and promote longevity. To reap these health benefits, you must give of yourself, which, as a shy person, you usually want to do, though you may hold back not to seem pushy.

One caveat: If you join a volunteer organization and your duties aren't defined, you may not feel needed. If that's the case, simply remind yourself that the organization is lucky to have your services and talents, which should help you move beyond your fears. Or, better yet, be proactive. Meet with or e-mail the group leader and ask for a project. If you're feeling bold, name your specific skills so that he or she can better find a suitable use for you within the organization. You'll feel less shy when your role is clearly defined.

Habit #2: Use the Internet—And Know When to Move to On

Among my nonshy clients, a popular strategy is to approach Internet dating as if they were job hunting. We'll discuss Internet dating in more detail in chapter ten, but briefly, many of these Nonshys regularly line up Internet dates and then incorporate a screening system to cut themselves loose from people they don't wish to see. One of my clients programs every Internet date's telephone number into her cell phone. If she's no longer interested in the person, she deletes his name and enters NO instead. Then, when NO appears on the readout, she just doesn't answer the phone. It might sound rude, but she feels she's in the business of finding a man to be her steady boyfriend. "I don't want to waste time on someone who doesn't qualify for the job," she said.

If that's too scary, you might try . . . scheduling your social life. Every week, take a look at your calendar and make it your mission to fill in at least one of your empty days or nights with a planned activity shared with friends or acquaintances you'd like to know better. Even if you're not spending time with a person to whom you're not romantically attached, you're honing your social skills. "If I stay in my apartment alone for too long, I tell myself that my social muscles are atrophying, and that motivates me to make dates with friends and people I'd like to get to know better," said Kayla, a twenty-nine-year-old merchandise buyer.

And what about cutting your losses, like my Internet-dating client? Typically, that isn't easy for shy singles. I've noticed that when many of my shy clients find someone to date, they tend to hang on, perhaps much longer then they should. "I dated Tom for two years before I finally called it quits because I miraculously met someone else," said Patricia, a shy single in her mid-twenties who had a long-distance relationship. It can be tough, but if you don't feel you're with the right person, you have to end it and move on (more on that in chapter seven).

If cutting your losses is too scary, you might try . . . keeping a journal or diary. It can help you build your case and convince yourself that breaking up with the person you're seeing is necessary. Overall, keeping a journal can be a powerful aide for addressing the difficulties of managing personal boundaries and loneliness, which may be holding you back from doing the deed. Many shy people don't take the time or invest the emotional energy to truly discern what they like and dislike; a daily journal, whether handwritten or typed, is a great tool for uncovering where you stand because your values, opinions, thoughts, and beliefs are presented in black and white.

Once you know where you stand and what your values are— whether "I don't want to date women who aren't Catholic," "I want to meet someone who wants to get married," or "I want to marry someone who doesn't want to change me"—the next challenge is having the courage to voice your position.

Habit #3: Entertain

Many of my nonshy clients frequently invite friends to their homes for parties and dinners. Or they arrange large restaurant get-togethers and invite people who don't know each other. They ask friends to bring one or two interesting people to round out the social scene because they know that if others bring new faces, their chances of meeting someone increase as well.

If that's too scary, you might try . . . entertaining in your home with an extroverted friend. Host smaller gatherings, which are more conducive to friendly, intimate conversation. Don't miss out on birthdays and other festive opportunities—use anything as an excuse for a celebration. Even an "It's spring!" tea or a Super Bowl party are great excuses for get-togethers. In fact, it's a good idea to invite people you're not romantically interested in at first, until you're more comfortable in the role of host.

Hosting becomes easier the more you do it. Prepare dishes ahead then heat them later so you won't spend all of your time in the kitchen. Or, better yet, give each guest a job, such as chopping cucumbers for the salad, so the focal point shifts from you to the tasks at hand. And to nurture an even greater sense of togetherness, which can further reduce your feelings of self-consciousness, plan activities you can do as a group, such as playing a board game. As you feel more comfortable hosting, include people you don't know well but might be interested in dating.

As a host, part of your responsibility is to initiate conversation. Although that can be an added stressor for the shy, there are strategies you might try. Everyone likes to tell stories that enhance their status or garner empathy or admiration. When you're sitting around the dinner table, encourage your guests by asking questions that play off funny or interesting tidbits they've mentioned or that you know about them, such as a recent promotion they've received, a vacation they just returned from, a chi-chi restaurant they've been to, or a sport in which they're active. (As you practice the skill of monitoring conversations for material, light bulbs will go off when conversational connectors come along.)

If things slow down during a dinner, feel free to shift the conversation's direction by throwing out more basic questions that stimulate your guests to talk about themselves, such as: "What's your favorite time of year?" or "What do you do in your spare time?" Try offering up something about yourself as well. For example: "I grew up in Kansas and never saw the ocean/mountains/desert before I moved here." Which could lead to, "How about you? Did you grow up here or somewhere else?" But don't feel it's your job to be the interviewer the entire time. Once the group conversation gets moving, feel free to back off and let it evolve on its own.

If you're milling about the cocktail party you're hosting, current events always offer good conversational segues. Prepare ahead of time by listening to the news or reading the newspaper and plant your question when the timing's right. "So, what did you do during the blackout?" Or, "Did you see the recent . . . ?" One of my shy clients who happens to be a good cook carries props as she "circulates" her parties, like a small platter of Vietnamese spring rolls. She offers them while peppering her guests with appropriate questions.

Habit #4: Ask Everyone You Know to Fix You Up

A popular technique among my nonshy clients is to ask coworkers, friends, and acquaintances, like their dentist and even their parents and their parents' friends, to introduce them to any good candidates they might know. The premise is that everybody is acquainted with someone, and who knows? It could be "the one." Of course, that individual could also be completely off—another person's idea of a "hottie" might not be the same as yours. So if you go the fix-up route, be willing to endure your share of near or complete misses. But because a mutual friend set you up, handle the situation with diplomacy. If you don't want to go out with the person again and she asks, try saying something like, "Let me check my calendar. I'm having a busy month." Then call (or leave a message), reiterating that you are, indeed, booked (you may just be seeing a friend). "But thanks anyway."

(For more strategies on how not to accept a second date, see chapter seven.)

If that's too scary, you might try . . . asking a select, trusted few to fix you up—those you know well and feel comfortable with, rather than friends of friends—and who know you well, too, such as a best friend, sibling, or other close relative. "It's embarrassing to admit you're looking," said Carla, a shy single in her late thirties who was too shy to ask others "if they knew someone." Still, she was able to network among her girlfriends at work and meet a man she likes, the first cousin of one of her office-mates.

Habit #5: Smile and Make Eye Contact

Many of my socially confident clients smile if they notice someone cute on the subway, in the elevator in their building, or at their job. If they see this person a second time, they say something like, "It looks like we're on the same schedule. My name is . . . And you?" Then, they follow up with a question, such as "Do you work (or live) in the building? I live (or work) on the seventeenth floor." The socially confident know that they often have to make the first move and be a bit forthcoming.

If that's too scary, you might try . . . starting small by making sure your day-to-day routine involves others. Try talking to strangers of all kinds, such as salesclerks, the man or woman

COACH'S CORNER

For general stress relief associated with shyness management, connect with nature to develop a sense of being part of a larger whole. Going for a leisurely walk in the park or sitting by a river and experiencing a sense of the sacredness of all things, like the splendor of a spring day or the divinity of a sunset, can ease stress and help put issues into perspective. Or, if you're more of an urban type, try going to a museum and communing with the masterpieces created by artistic geniuses. That may also offer the uplifting sense that anything is possible and help you imagine what your future might hold.

behind the dry-cleaning counter, the mailperson, or other parents at your children's school. The goal isn't ultimately to date them; it's to become comfortable talking to people you don't know well. A simple question, such as "How are you?" as you're paying for groceries or holding the door, or even just smiling and saying hello, can provide a background of positive social interactions. The courage history you build through these small steps can help you take it a degree further and begin talking to an interesting-looking stranger who crosses your path.

Habit # 6: Learn to Laugh at Yourself

Dating has a serious side, and it should. After all, how you socialize in this arena and the decisions you make regarding it may affect your destiny. Still, many of my nonshy singles don't take their personal lives too solemnly. They try to see the lighter side of a situation and chalk it up to experience, even if it's grim or embarrassing. "After a first date with someone I was really interested in, I discovered that I had a poppy seed lodged between my front teeth—from the dressing on my salad," said Sean, a forty-one-year-old construction manager. "And to think that all evening I was trying to be Mr. Perfect," he said. "I just had to laugh." Indeed, humor can even help diffuse the three stages of a shyness attack.

If that's too scary, you might try . . . imagining how boring life would be if everything was perfect or went according to plan. Just keep trying to see the ironic side of life and perhaps develop friendships with people who can laugh at themselves. Let them be your role models.

Habit #7: Come Prepared with Strategies

You'd be surprised at how much preparation some of my nonshy singles do before a big date or an important party. They think up topics of conversation to initiate, such as current events, recent movies, or books on the best-seller list they've read, and even rehearse their "opening" until it feels comfortable. When things are up and running, they constantly mine the conversation, facial expressions, and the scene for important details to guide their comments and actions. If things stall, they try another topic in their repertoire. In essence, their focus is directed outward, and they hope for the best. In fact, they *expect* that others will respond positively to them. "When I get the cold shoulder, I just assume she was in a bad mood or that she didn't feel like talking," said Samuel, a Nonshy in his twenties who uses that technique to "fake out failure."

If that's too scary, you might try . . . thinking up one topic to discuss that's related to current events. Also, simply reassure yourself that you're with a colleague or a friend (your date), not an adversary, and breathe, breathe, breathe through it all. You're bound to enjoy yourself more, even if no sparks fly.

One of my clients, Katrina, a "closet shy" physician, who, according to all outward appearances, seems extremely social, invented two strategies that boost her confidence and help her manage high-profile social events. She devised one as a child and the other as an adult, which she calls her "adult social boldness card."

First, can you guess why she changed her name from Mary as a shy six-year-old? (Her parents let her start calling herself Katrina, which she adopted from a children's book, and it stuck.) Even at that tender age she believed the new name made her less invisible, which, as you know, is a common symptom of shyness. I'm not suggesting that you change your name if you like yours, but you might if you don't feel it best represents you. A few years ago, another shy client of mine stopped going by his given first name, Leslie; instead, he went by John, his middle name, when he started a new job because he felt John was more dignified. "I've been John ever since, and I feel better about me," he said.

Katrina devised her second shyness management tactic for

"beautiful people" events—you know, the kind of social events where everyone is taller, more in shape, and more attractive than you think you are. Katrina is often invited to such high-profile social functions because she's on the board of directors at a prominent hospital in New York City. Before such a party, Katrina prepares by reminding herself of specific events throughout her day in which she felt "tall" in her office, like when she accurately diagnosed a patient or ran a successful office meeting. Then, when she walks into a difficult social scene, she's emotionally armed with her "tall" memories, which help her begin to talk easily. This strategy can work for all types of events, not just major to-dos. Before any shindig you're attending, ask yourself, *When did I feel "tall" (or fit or beautiful) during my day?* You could even write a code phrase on a piece of paper, such as "office meeting," and keep it handy in your pocket or purse for quick, on-the-spot reference, to remind yourself throughout the evening.

YOUR ACTION PLAN

The strategies I discuss to combat each stage of a shyness attack, such as practicing active listening (page 69–70), talking briefly about yourself (page 71), and cutting yourself some slack (pages 97–98), can also strengthen your social confidence skills. Take a moment now to compose a comprehensive list of four or five techniques and put them on your social-confidence-building "to do" list. (You might list your number-one and -two ranked strategies from chapters three, four, and five.) Focus on the behaviors that will help you manage the stage of a shyness attack that's giving you the most trouble at the moment. To that list, add any from this chapter that sound doable

Which core confidence-building strategies (or their less scary variations) will you try? Record your action plan in the space on page 116. Consider photocopying your plan for easy reference when you're dating.

I'd like to try to boost my confidence by:

_____

_____

_____

_____

_____

_____

_____

_____

_____

_____

_____

_____

COACH'S CORNER

Another powerful confidence-building technique is to keep a pen and paper by your bed. Before going to sleep each night, write down a minimum of ten good things you did that day, no matter how trivial. Begin each sentence with "I." For example: *I smiled at the doorman* or *I invited two friends over for coffee on Saturday afternoon.* By focusing on each day's successes, you'll program yourself to stay motivated and positive, because the essence of social confidence and optimism is succeeding at something. And remember, small victories can add up big.

Remember to tackle just one strategy at a time before moving on to the next. And congratulate yourself as you progress. If you experience a setback—during one of your strategies, for example, a negative inner voice creeps in, such as 'It's no use, I'm just not cut out for this'—defuse it by agreeing with it on the spot. In other words, concede that, of course, you're shy and that confidence building is tough. Then you'll be free to focus on what you're feeling and what you're going to do about it instead of getting sucked into a vortex of self-loathing.

WHAT'S YOUR COURAGE SCORE?

We complete this chapter with your courage score. On a scale of 1 to 10, with 1 being the courage of a kitten (you rarely make eye contact with strangers), and 10 the courage of a lion (you ask everyone you know to fix you up), rate your confidence-building courage score. Circle your score below.

```
1  1.5  2  2.5  3  3.5  4  4.5  5  5.5  6  6.5  7  7.5  8  8.5  9  9.5  10
```

You may wish to write your score in the space that follows: _____

If your courage score is more kitten than lion—perhaps it's 3.5—ask yourself what steps you can incorporate from your action plans to increase your score to 4, and add them to this chapter's action plan. Challenge yourself in the coming weeks to raise your courage score one half point at a time by, for example, inviting a group of friends over for a holiday cocktail party. They're just friends, but still, it's a chance to flex your social biceps. Whatever you decide to try will help you get that much closer to liberating self-awareness and that much further from crippling self-consciousness. Since this chapter focuses on the habits of the socially confident, by definition your courage may pale in comparison to Nonshys, but keep returning to your action plan. With every small step you take, conscious movement fosters unconscious momentum.

{SEVEN}

FIRST DATES: WHAT COMES AFTER HELLO

IF YOU'RE SHY AROUND PEOPLE YOU DON'T KNOW, a first date can be one of the most awkward social situations you can encounter as an adult. Not only are you forced to talk at length with someone you just met, you may also be physically attracted to that person at first glance. Under such "loaded" conditions, many of my shy clients report feeling sweaty, faint, nervous, removed, or withdrawn. "When I asked Kelly to have dinner with me, I felt as if I were having an out-of-body experience," said Todd. Still, by this stage in his quest to manage dating-related shyness, Todd knew he deserved to pat himself on the back for having the courage to actually ask Kelly for a date. It's common to avoid uncomfortable feelings by either talking yourself out of doing the asking, which Todd had a history of, or only asking out or accepting dates from those you're not that attracted to. (Sound familiar?) Although initially bearable, very safe people can become uninspiring; it's like accepting a job for which you sense you're overqualified. On day one, you're already comfortable. By day five, you're kicking yourself because you didn't aim higher. The same often goes for dating below your emotional

118

reach. On the other hand, if you feel awkward or uncomfortable at some point, this could be a sign that you are out of your comfort zone—and possibly experiencing sexual tension (more on that a little later).

Overall, just being in the dating ballpark makes Shys feel awkward or uncomfortable, at least initially. Some of my shy clients have no problem asking a person out, but they clam up during the actual date. Others are terrified of issuing the invitation by phone or even e-mail and simply wait for the potential new acquaintance to make the first move. Some have trouble with both. Whatever your first-date stumbling block, keep in mind that it's only a date and that the first time for anything is challenging just because it's new. But first dates do get easier—from asking or accepting the date, to experiencing it, to saying goodnight when it's over. The key is to learn to manage the stages of a shyness attack that typically interfere. This chapter contains suggestions that my shy clients have found helpful in making first dates easier at every step. Some of the tips are actually contradictory—but because we're all different, try approaching the challenge from several angles.

MAKING THE DATE

When you ask someone out, you certainly don't *want* to get "No" for an answer. But occasionally, "no" happens to everyone. Even though it can sting, getting a "no"—just as much as getting a "yes"—is a sign that you're a player in the dating game. With that in mind, here's an either-or strategy for plucking up the courage to ask someone out. These contradictory defenses work in different ways for different people and in different situations.

To soften the fear of initiation so you can actually utter the invitation, try accepting that asking for a first date is scary. Come clean with yourself (*I'm nervous—I do care what happens*) and acknowledge the challenge of doing the asking—instead of doing the opposite and pretending you're not afraid. This can help dissipate the fear so it doesn't overwhelm you. You'll avoid wasting time and energy if denial tends to create an obstacle between you and your goal. Keep in mind that getting your armor up by downplaying your fear could make you feel *more* fearful and conflicted if that's *not* how you truly feel. "I used to tell myself before I asked a woman out, 'I'm cool. I do this all the time,'" said Ted, a shy single who had been interested in a woman at work for a while. "Then I started saying, 'Cut it out, Ted. You're a mess. Admit it.' Amazingly, I began to feel less uptight. Pardon the cliché, but the truth set me free," he grinned. Ted realized that giving himself permission to acknowledge what he felt was a form of self-support—paradoxically, it created inner confidence, and it showed. When he finally asked out the woman, she said yes. This "call a spade a spade" technique may work for you, too, on some occasions; the only way to know for sure is to try it.

If the strategy of honesty doesn't calm you, try doing the opposite, employing the defense of denial. Remember the Italian movie *Life Is Beautiful*, in which the father pretends to his son that the concentration camp they're in is only a game. This ploy helped them both endure it. It may also work for you, too, with first dates. For example, one of my shy singles is fond of telling himself: "It's another date. Big deal. I've been on plenty of them. Women are like socks—I have to change them frequently." His bravado has earned him a nickname among his friends; they call him "Socks." Of course, deep down he's nervous. But tossing dates into the "take a number" category seems to help him calm his nerves and get through it.

Asking the Question

Once you find the method that brings you to the starting gate, you can then work up to inviting your potential date. Begin with small talk, such as current events, how was that person's day, the weather, or a movie you recently saw. If this task is like climbing Mt. Everest, try the preparation strategies I suggest throughout this book. For a few days before you ask, flex your small-talk muscles by practicing on strangers. Ask for directions, offer assistance to hold doors, and smile and say something simple like "hello" to as many people as you can. This strategy builds surprising momentum.

COACH'S CORNER

In a group situation, be sure to bolster your confidence with the strategies from previous chapters; otherwise, you run the large risk of losing the boldness to speak to the person you want and getting lost in the crowd. Groups can be good for getting an "in," but they can also work against you when it comes to having meaningful conversation.

When it comes time to actually ask for the date, I often advise my clients *not* to blatantly say, "Would you like to go out (with me) this weekend?" because if it's a "no" answer, it often feels like full-on rejection. If the person declines for whatever reason, it can easily appear as if he or she just doesn't want to go out with *you*, because there was nothing else offered to reject but you. Instead, hedge your bets (and protect your ego) by leading with the *event* part of the date. For example, "A friend gave me special tickets to (something). Would you like to go?" is a strategy for asking someone out that removes you from the core of the invitation. That something might be a lecture, a concert, a movie, a play, a museum exhibit, or a sporting event. If your potential date says, "No, thanks," she may be disinterested in the something, not you. (It's perfectly fine to tell yourself that.) Or you might say, "Someone like you is probably taken, but if not, I happen to have tickets for . . . " That gives your date two outs that aren't about rejecting you. She could say, "You're right, I am taken," or, "Thanks, but I've already seen that play."

If you get any form of a "no," take a deep cleansing breath and try turning that response into a counterproposal: "Well, how about next week? Is that better for you?" If she's still not available and doesn't say when she is, let it go. As they say, nothing ventured, nothing gained. You have added to your life experi-

ence by giving yourself the opportunity to tolerate "no" without
any disaster.

To soften the blow of first-date rejection, remind yourself
ahead of time that you control the asking. You have absolutely
no control over the person you're asking out. You can't make
her say yes, but you can issue an invitation and see what happens. If she says no, tell yourself, *Okay, so I asked*, give yourself
credit for taking that bold step, then say *Next!* to yourself, and
move on. Keep in mind that a rejection could easily reflect a
problem that may have much more to do with the other person
than you. Your job isn't to psychoanalyze someone you don't
know or chastise yourself for getting turned down. Your mission
is to celebrate your courage. You asked someone out. Bravo!

Another option, if the object of your affection is someone you
already know or you're familiar with his circle of peers, is to invite others who are close to him to an art opening, sports bar, or
any group encounter, and then suggest that your potential date
be included. Or, skirt the issue entirely and entertain at home
with several friends on the occasion of a holiday, an Oscar or
Super Bowl party, or a birthday. Say, "I'm having several people
over on Saturday night. If you're available, here's my address. It's casual. . . ."

In the midst of this en-
counter, listen carefully for
ways to casually insert yourself
into his or her life. You might,
for example, volunteer to assist
in installing his new computer
or hooking up her new DVD
player. Or you could try something basic like, "You like
classic/Coen brothers/foreign
films, too? We should catch
one at the classic/cult/art house

COACH'S CORNER

In addition to listening for conversational cues as an entrée
into a discussion, timing is also
an important factor. Be mindful
of the topic before breaking
in. If he's talking about a sensitive subject, you wouldn't, for
example, interject, "I couldn't
help but overhear that you were
just fired. What kind of work did
you do?" If it requires that you
step away and come back to
him in a few minutes for a fresh
start, so much the better for
picking up this clue.

theatre sometime." That leaves it open-ended for him or her to say, "Yeah, that'd be great," and either walk away or follow up. Either way, the invitation is extended, and you save face.

Role Reversal

These days, women ask men out, and there's pressure from the media and from other nonshy women to take that step. "Why don't you just call him?" many Nonshys urge their friends. If only. Asking men out can be especially tough if you're a shy female because there's still a long-standing social expectation that men step up to the plate. "The one time I tried asking out a guy, I felt so devalued when I actually stammered out the question. After all, if he wanted to go out with me, wouldn't he have asked?" said Grace, a thirty-something biologist. "Anyway, he said no because he had a race the next day that he needed to rest up for—after all, he was a runner. That may have been true, but I never asked out a guy again," she said. "But I have to admit, when I think about it, I did feel good to be the one taking action."

Women have made their mark in dozens of traditionally male careers, from construction worker to presidential cabinet member. Still, they're often the ones waiting for the phone to ring or the e-mails to appear. It doesn't have to be that way. If you want to be more proactive, the theater tickets and "you probably have a girlfriend" tactics can work for you, too. But remember that if the answer is no, men get rejected all the time, and it doesn't put *them* off. So, keep trying. (I suggested to Grace that she try again.)

ACCEPTING OR REJECTING A FIRST DATE

If you're in the position of accepting a first date, remember to convey your enthusiasm ("That sounds great—I'd love to"), even if you're reticent about going on the date itself. If you appear less than excited simply because you're wary of this new experience, you may unwittingly tap into the other person's insecurities, which can start the relationship on a sour note. A long pause or monotone answer in response to being asked out may trigger negative emotions others have about being boring or uninteresting. As a shy person, especially, you want to be particularly sensitive about inducing feelings of awkwardness and discomfort in others. Just keep in mind that even if your date doesn't seem shy, he may have had to muster up courage to ask you out.

Conversely, if you don't want to go out with someone who asks, you may have a difficult time declining, especially if the person who asks is very persistent. "I just couldn't say no when Joe called me," said Marcelle, an administrative assistant in publishing. "I wasn't that interested, but I couldn't think of a way to turn him down without hurting his feelings." Indeed, if you're shy and aware of rejection, you might try to avoid inflicting that particular pain on others. A good exit strategy is to say, "My week's pretty backed up. Let me check my calendar." Then call or leave a message to say that you are booked but "thanks anyway." If he asks you out for a different day, say that date doesn't look good either; hopefully he'll get the message. But don't offer false hope ("maybe next week"), unless you feel you really might change your mind. If this is a person you see often—maybe he works in your office or goes to the same gym—make sure that whatever answer you give him will not prove to be a blatant lie, such as saying you're on deadline when you're really out with others from the office that night. Your best option is to be honest and say, or e-mail, something like, "I

COACH'S CORNER

Of course, if you were the one asking for a date and received a no, your preference would probably be to know why you were turned down, but you'd also prefer not to be shamed. In the spirit of not doing to another person what you don't want done to you, always balance honesty with humanity; help the asker to save face and feel good about himself for taking the risk and asking by not going into detail ("You're not my type." "I don't like men with bellies." "I prefer blondes."). If you feel a reason is necessary, offer what you believe is the softest blow.

just don't get the sense that we're right for each other, and I don't want to waste your time."

But sometimes it's a good idea to go against the tide and expand your boundaries: If the person asking you out is adamant, you might consider giving him a shot. "When David called, I mentioned that I had a boyfriend to scare him away," said Isabella, a shy single in her early thirties. "David said, 'If you have a boyfriend, then where is he?' I thought, he's right. I was wondering the same thing myself. My boyfriend was a ghost. He never called when he said he would and left me hanging on the weekends," she said. Isabella gave David a chance. She allowed herself to be open to the possibility that someone she wasn't initially wild about might actually be her Mr. Right. Isabella began to enjoy her time with him very much and decided that her original impression was based on very limited knowledge of who he was. It's a real pleasure when someone turns out to be an unexpected gem.

COACH'S CORNER

An essential aspect of dating is flexing your personal power—to be able to bend or break your own rules when you intentionally and consciously determine that's the right plan. It's a very different action than being completely malleable, with no strong opinion of your own—saying, for example, "Sure, I'm not doing anything on Friday," when what you really mean is "but I still don't want to go out with you." Rather, when you flex your personal power, you're calling the shots and evaluating them as you go.

GOING ON THE DATE

To help overcome dating inhibitions, particularly if stage two is a problem for you, think carefully about the venue for the first date. The conventional drinks-and-dinner date is fine for the nonshy, but for some shy singles who come to my groups, it can be very difficult. "It's too easy to feel like you're in the limelight," said Tina, a computer consultant in her early forties. "You feel like every move you make—from taking a sip of your drink to how your chew your lettuce—is under the microscope." If you're like Tina, better first-date venues for you might feature non-threatening situations in which you're casually and publicly *doing something* with others, like rollerblading in the park, playing tennis, or walking around a zoo.

Some Shys get around first-date pressure by naming it something else. "On our 'first date,' I taught Rebecca how to drive a stick shift," said Scott, a shy engineer. Under the premise of driving lessons, they got to know each other, and one day they discovered they were dating, even though they hadn't yet spent one evening being waited on. "We stayed out of restaurants until our third 'date,' when we were more comfortable with each other," Scott said.

Whatever you decide to do, if you know you become stymied by freezing or are prone to flooding, prepare by reviewing the strategies I introduced in chapter four in case of awkward moments. Some of the strategies that readily apply to first dates include naming stage two while it's happening. If you notice, for example, that you're talking a lot or not talking enough, silently admit, *Okay, I'm experiencing stage two, but it will pass*, to help yourself detach from the fear that's grabbed ahold of you. You might also repeat a self-affirming mantra, such as *I'm an interesting person. I have a lot to offer*, to calm yourself and drown out other negative self-talk you may be "hearing" under the pressure of the situation. Also, consider the following first-date pointers for anticipating and alleviating any awkwardness.

First Date Dos

- **Dress well.** For a first date (and, really, subsequent dates), choose clothes that make you feel beautiful, handsome, sexy, and free. This might seem like an obvious bit of advice, but your appearance can provide you with "props" that aid the conversational flow and bolster your confidence from the outside in. As I mentioned earlier, consider wearing a "signature" pair of earrings, hairstyle, or shade of lipstick—or pocket square, bow tie, or watch—that can trigger conversation about how you got it, where you found it, or who gave it to you.

- **Breathe.** And breathe again. This is a concept worth repeating. If you're in the grip of stage two, and babbling is your tendency, resist the urge to fill the void or interrupt when your date is talking. Take several deep breaths instead. If your forte is to freeze up, try turning your date's words or phrases into a question, such as "You grew up in Idaho? What was that like?" People love to talk about themselves. Intently listening to your date conveys interest and generates goodwill. Listening is an underrated virtue; it makes others feel valued.

- **Come prepared.** As in other social situations, think up a list of reasonable, activity-specific questions to casually pose to your date to get her talking so you have something to respond to. Then listen with openness and add your own two cents, when appropriate, disclosing something human about yourself that doesn't reveal too much personal information. For instance, if you're ice-skating, you could say, "This is great. I haven't ice-skated since I was a kid. Have you?" If you're visiting an Egyptian museum exhibit, you might say, "I've only starting learning about the pyramids from the History Channel. Have you been interested in them for a while?" Revealing personal details indicates a willingness to be open. Sensing your generosity, your date may offer her own self-disclosure and voilà!—you're conversing.

- **Cut yourself (and your date) some slack.** A multitude of my shy clients are impossible to please, though they may perceive themselves as just the opposite. Their dates are never good enough. "What can I say? I'm picky," admitted Jennifer, a shy writer in her late forties. She's not alone. Many of the shy singles I've worked with have the tendency to find fatal flaws in their suitors before they've had their first sip of Chardonnay or ordered their cappuccino. They silently criticize their dates for such things as talking too slowly or quickly, not knowing how to order at Starbucks, or using their napkin as a Kleenex. Because Shys are highly critical of themselves, few people can meet their standards, especially if they show interest in them. To Shys, Groucho Marx's famous line, "I'd never want to be in a club that would have me as a member," isn't such a joke.

Think about it. If you can't accept yourself, how can you give others the benefit of the doubt? If that sounds like you, I urge you to dig deeply, turn the tables, and consider how your own lack of self-acceptance may actually be interfering with your ability to accept and love others. Self-kindness and awareness, free of self-criticism, increase your chances of making emotional space in your life for others. Jennifer, for example, learned to distinguish characteristics about her first dates that truly annoyed her from those that were a reflection of her own self-criticism by making a mental list of things she found annoying about her date afterwards. "Then, I divide the list into two categories: 'things that may have more to do with me than him,' such as 'he ordered steak' (I'm an aspiring vegetarian), and 'legitimate complaints,' such as 'he chews with his mouth open.' Then I focus on my own shortcomings to gauge whether I can live with what I perceive to be his legitimate ones. My line of reasoning may go along the lines of, 'Do I chew with my mouth open? Well, not that I know of. But maybe I do. And even if I don't, perhaps this habit can be fixed down the line with gentle reminders.' Generally, I weigh the good with the bad to come up with a more realistic assessment of whether I want to continue dating the person," she said. Jennifer's system seems to be

COACH'S CORNER

To ease first-date jitters, hold a mental rehearsal before the event. Picture yourself during the date: sitting across from the other person in a coffee shop, laughing at a comedy club, or having fun strolling through a street fair. The images we have in our minds are the templates for our "performances." Just visualizing yourself relaxed increases the chances that you'll feel mellower when the time comes.

working. "I've gone on a lot more second dates than I ever had before this strategy," she noted.

COACH'S CORNER

Acknowledging to yourself your own shortcomings during a first date could free you to focus on how you feel about your date and the overall experience. The first date (and subsequent dates) will likely be much more pleasant—for both of you.

· **Highlight mutual interests.** Discovering that someone you're attracted to likes the same things you do can be exciting. You have an instant common bond, a little bit of emotionally validating Velcro, that may help a relationship "stick." So when you learn about your shared interests, speak up instead of just keeping them to yourself. An example: "I can't believe you like to cook, too. Most of my friends just go out to eat. What do you enjoy making?" It's refreshing to meet a kindred spirit.

· **Tell it like it is.** An obvious strategy is to say, "Okay, I confess. I'm shy," to help your date better understand your reactions and relieve your stress level. The typical response is often "So am I" or "You don't seem shy." "When I told Martha I was shy, she said, 'Really?'" said Charlie, a shy single in his late twenties. "Then she recounted all the things I had done that didn't seem shy— from asking her out to sending her a 'looking forward to our date' e-mail. I had to convince her I was. It also made me realize that maybe I'm not as shy as I thought I was, or at least, I can fake it if I need to." In any event, the more you're able to put your feelings into words, the less likely you'll enact them in a way that isn't your conscious intention. Giving voice to our fears can be liberating.

Other Tips for a First Date

· If you wear something that's totally not you, like four-inch Manolo Blahniks when you're really a Birkenstock kind of woman, or something that's brand new and "untested," you can wind up feeling self-conscious or like you're someone you're not—for example, when your blouse gapes (who knew?), your toes pinch, or the waist proves too tight and uncomfortable.

· Usually when you're getting to know someone, you want to be open but not confessional—not laying too much on the line. Helen, an Internet executive in her early thirties and self-described "flooder," learned that truth the hard way. "The fact that I was illegitimate, that I was raised in a foster home for much of my childhood, that my foster parents spent our grocery money on alcohol, and as a result, I often went to bed hungry— all of that used to come out on a first date, especially if my date was a good listener—because it was cathartic, and it's very much a part of who I am," she said. "But after scaring a lot of dates away, I've learned to save those details for later, after I've really gotten to know someone. In my case, I sounded like a fixer-upper, which can be burdensome." She's not wrong. In most situations, it's usually wiser to save your war stories for later. Remember, you're only on a first date. If things work out, you'll have time for more revealing conversation later.

· From what I gather, "how tough it is out there" is a common bonding topic among shy and nonshy singles alike. But keep in mind that discussing your dating game plan, as well as who else you've dated, might be unappealing. "It's tempting to talk about all the strategies you're trying, especially if you're going for something novel, like speed dating or the Internet for the first time," said Paul, a twenty-seven-year-old insurance salesman. Burdened with too much information, though, your date may emotionally pull away. "My date asked about my work and seemed to be listening," said Denise, an accountant in her early fifties, recounting one first date. "Then he confided that he, too, was dating online." It was downhill from there. Denise soon learned how many e-mails her date liked to send, how quickly he asks a woman out, and details about one woman who hadn't said yes to going out with him. "I thought, 'Check please!'" said Denise, "but I didn't

have the guts. I just sat there and listened, like I was his therapist. Ugh."

On first dates, make it your usual policy to *not* talk about
dating—there will be time for personal history later. Delving into
such personal territory so soon can squash a new relationship.
Proceed with caution if your date brings it up.

Saying Goodnight

For some Shys, ending a first date can be as challenging as
asking for or accepting it. Regardless of whether they've taken a
liking to the person, they worry about how the date will end, because a first date can often be the beginning of a physical relationship. "The proverbial kiss goodnight at the front door is
always a nagging concern for me," said Rose, a twenty-nine-year-
old computer programmer. "I worry about whether it's expected
and whether I should."

Here, like with other aspects of dating, it pays to have a
policy. Some of my clients never kiss any of their first dates because a premature intimate interlude could usher them into days
of payback and remorse. Instead, they wave and say goodbye, re-
serving physical contact for future encounters, when they're
more sure of themselves and of the possibility of a love connection. Others keep their options open, based on what transpires
during the date. Remember, you're in control of how you handle
your end of the deal.

If you're unsure of where
you stand on the nightcap
issue, address it by keeping a
journal to establish your personal sexual boundaries. Answer such questions as: *How
did I feel when I got in over my
head sexually before I was ready:
That night? The next day? Sev-*

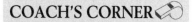

COACH'S CORNER

It's a good strategy to picture
how you want the first date to
conclude. Be specific about
speech and body language. If
it's clearly developed in your
mind, you will increase the
chances of avoiding serious mis-
understandings.

eral days later? What was the relationship like after that? As I mentioned in chapter six, the beauty of keeping a journal is that you have direct, concrete evidence of what you think and feel about your personal limits. By writing them down, you'll make your sexual and other dating policies real, and you'll be less likely to veer from that written path when the time comes.

R$_X$ FOR FIRST DATES

To help you better manage first-date shyness, zero in on the most problematic aspects of first dates you've been on. Was it the initial getting-to-know-you chitchat? Were there long pauses in the conversation? Was it saying goodbye? Or the fact that you accepted the date in the first place? Remember how you've felt, either when asking for or accepting the date, during the experience itself, and when your shyness overcame you.

First dates are particularly challenging for me when:

Now, to help you move forward, ask, *What did I do in the past that didn't work?* and *What can I do differently in the future?* Write your answers in the space below and on the next page.

_____

_____

_____

_____

_____

_____

_____

SECOND DATES

Assuming you had a good time and want to see the person again, vying for a second date can be even harder than asking for the first, especially if the first was a set-up. What to do? Lead with something you learned about the person on the first date. Did she mention that she likes to swing dance? Then ask her to a dance club that gives free lessons. Does he like to bike ride? Then suggest going cycling together on a scenic local bike trail. If nothing else, you'll get brownie points for being a good listener.

If you didn't do the asking the first time around but would like to go out again, when saying goodnight, you might:

- Add, "I had a really great time. Do you want to get together next week?" (Note: Don't request the next date for the following day.)

- Think of something else you'd like to do with your date and come up with a game plan. If you want to avoid an intimate, and potentially uncomfortable or embarrassing, conversation, call your date when he's at work (on the first workday after the date) and thank him for the great time. Then briefly propose your game plan.

- Throw caution to the wind and call her at home the next day to say thanks for the date and invite her for another.

- Once you're home, call and leave a message on his machine to say thanks and that you're looking forward to going out again sometime—it'll be the first thing he hears when he gets home.

If you don't want to go out a second time, you may have difficulty saying no thanks, especially if your date is interested in you. A good strategy is to be honest. If he wants an immediate answer, tell him you'll check your calendar. But the next day, simply leave a message or drop him an e-mail saying that you had a pleasant evening but you don't want to lead him on. And, with slight modifications, several of the first-date rejection techniques that I outlined on pages 124–125 work just as well when declining a second invitation.

IF YOU EXPERIENCE PAYBACK

Because first dates tend to make shy singles feel vulnerable, especially if they're attracted to the person, first-date payback is one of the most popular topics among the members of my shyness groups and workshops. Like a heat-seeking missile, they're expert at homing in on and playing back every perceived fatal flaw that came to bear throughout the date—from how they danced or responded to questions or didn't respond to things that seem funny in retrospect. Gregory, a salesman in his early forties, said, "At the door, my date tried to kiss me on the cheek. But when I saw it coming, I anticipated her move and we ended up bobbing heads." Gregory cringed for days over that one.

When I hear workshop participants recount their first-date imperfections, it can be heartrending and/or funny—if the speaker is willing to see the humor of the situation. They want to be Mr. or Ms. Perfect themselves. But life doesn't run smoothly for anyone. And by focusing so intently on themselves, they can miss the opportunity to ask some serious questions, such as "Did I like that person? Would I go out with her again?" "What did I like about him most?" Even if that first date doesn't progress to another one, the experience can help you learn about yourself and the qualities you're looking for in a potential mate. Don't deprive yourself of what you should consider valuable research by only focusing on "what went wrong."

Here are some ideas to stop punishing yourself and start realistically assessing the situation instead. For more on curtailing payback, review the tips in chapter five that start on page 92.

1. Review the Paybacker's Creed on page 99. It can come in handy after a first date, too. Many shy singles find first dates are a good time to reread it. "I keep a copy of the Paybacker's Creed in my bedroom drawer so I can get it out in the middle of the night," admitted Kurt, a shy single in his early thirties whose "worst payback time" tormented him when he was trying to fall asleep after a date.

2. Recognize payback while it's happening. As soon as you feel yourself getting upset or embarrassed over the way the date unfolded, label it. And remember to be wary of superior-sounding self-talk.

3. Give yourself permission to obsess less and less. If you can't prevent brutal first-date payback, limit it. Gradually, it will lose its bite, and the urge to reenact the alleged "crime" will dissipate.

4. Cut yourself some slack. You're only human. Remember, it's our imperfections that make us interesting, exciting, vulnerable, and approachable. Like other singles you meet, you deserve patience and understanding. For example, if you're reflecting on a conversational moment when there was an uncomfortable silence, instead of attacking yourself, your inner dialogue could sound like this: "I felt so uncomfortable for both of us. Ah, well. We got through it." And consider the alternative. If you didn't go out on first dates, you wouldn't learn and get better at dating. The more you date, the easier it gets.

5. If, despite your best intentions, your negative inner voice speaks from time to time, go with the flow. Agree with it. For example, concede that yes, you've got flaws. You don't

feel comfortable on first dates. You wish you'd talk more (or less), or could reliably think of something clever to say, or whatever. You may be surprised how liberating agreeing with that voice can be. "'So I'm not perfect,' is what I usually end up saying to myself. 'What else is new?'" chuckled Adam, a database manager at a law firm. That conclusion helped Adam move on. "I spend much less time criticizng myself these days," he said.

YOUR ACTION PLAN

Which strategies will you try on your next first date? Record your game plan in the space that follows. Consider photocopying it for easy reference.

The next time I have a first date, I'd like to try to manage my shyness by:

WHAT'S YOUR COURAGE SCORE?

We complete this chapter with your courage score. On a scale of 1 to 10, with 1 being the courage of a kitten (you declined several first date invitations over some period of time), and 10 the courage of a lion (you went on at least one first date this month), rate your first-date courage score. Circle your score below.

1 1.5 2 2.5 3 3.5 4 4.5 5 5.5 6 6.5 7 7.5 8 8.5 9 9.5 10

You may wish to write your score in the space that follows: _____

If your courage score is more kitten than lion—perhaps it's 4—ask yourself what you can incorporate from your action plan to increase your score to 4.5. When a first date arises, try to bring your courage score up another half point by attempting—or even imagining—one of the steps suggested in this and previous chapters. For example, let's say you refuse to allow your aunt to fix you up with a man who works in her office. For a .5 increase in courage, you could agree to at least listen to why she thinks this man may be a good date for you. Now that's not so difficult, is it?

"Never let the fear of striking out get in your way."

—*Babe Ruth*

{EIGHT}

HANDLING EXTREME DATING TERRAIN

RIGHT UP THERE WITH FIRST DATES are three other social roles that present particular obstacles for Shys; emotionally, they can be akin to rock climbing without a spotter. They include going solo to a wedding or dinner party where a lot of couples will attend; asking your partner where the relationship is going; and either rejecting or being rejected. Although these shyness-challenging scenarios may seem disparate, surviving them requires adopting the same basic philosophy of learned optimism, a concept developed by Martin Seligman, Ph.D., in his aptly titled book *Learned Optimism*. In this process of transforming negative or fearful attitudes and behaviors into positive ones, you mindfully undertake specific actions that influence a shift towards joy. Similarly, throughout *The Shy Single*, I promote a healthy dose of positivism in the form of courage-building exercises to help you tackle each stage of a shyness attack. In this chapter, however, I take learned optimism a step further by delving into the tactical aspects of negotiating three real-world confidence rockers that require an extra dose of resolve to survive them with both self-esteem and confidence intact.

138

THE WEDDING GUEST

"How can I make friends when everyone comes ensconced in their own cozy cocoon?" said Sheila, a shy single in her early thirties who had been to many weddings where she felt like the odd woman out. "It's impossible," added Rick, a divorced father in his early fifties. Can you think of worse places to be, if you're a shy single, than at weddings or dinner parties attended primarily by couples? What makes these gatherings so potentially alienating is that during the event, you may find yourself stranded and self-conscious.

"I was doing fine at the wedding until everyone got up to dance," said André, who admitted that at this juncture in the evening, he just sat at his table, alone, fiddling with the olive in his cocktail. "It wasn't too bad when everyone was dancing, but when they started to come back to the table, I wanted to hide. I might as well have had a neon sign that said LOSER over my head," he said. Many in the workshop that evening nodded in "been there" agreement. It's a difficult situation. Still, there were several things André might have done to lessen his embarrassment, which I'll outline in the action plan below; these pointers may be useful in case you ever find yourself in a similar situation.

Your Single-among-Couples Action Plan

First, tell yourself that instead of feeling miserably alone, you're going to devote yourself to noticing who else might need a friendly chat. This technique is helpful in managing the fear of initiation and the freezing or flooding that defines stage two. As soon as you arrive at the wedding or dinner, begin your project. Look around for someone who is also by themselves. Try approaching that person and introducing yourself. To prepare yourself for this ambitious goal, think about it before leaving for the evening, or during the drive over. Some of my shy single clients, even if they're not sure they'll be outnumbered, write themselves a script entitled "How I'm Going to Survive This Event if It's Mostly Couples." They then jot down a bulleted "to do" list that involves approaching others. In short, instead of playing the lone single at a mostly couples shindig, they reassign themselves the role of social facilitator.

This tactic works because nothing stops loneliness and self-consciousness faster than thinking of how you can help another person. Altruism is mightier than the underlying fear that fuels a shyness attack. True, self-consciousness can be readily triggered during an event if you *feel* like the odd person out, even though you may not seem that way to others. But by assigning yourself the role of Social Nightingale, you can resuscitate an outing that's on the respirator. It gives you something to do that's self-less and dignified—and much healthier and more productive than hovering in the restroom, for example, or trying to extract the pimento from your martini olive.

COACH'S CORNER

When you're single at a couple's event, think of someone you know who pulls off the inter-esting-single-person routine well. "I have a zany aunt who traveled the world and never got married," said Judith, a shy single in her early forties, who also liked traveling but did hope for marriage to the right man someday. "When I'm at couples' events, I use her as my role model. And I even say to myself, 'Okay, Judith. Get a grip. What would Aunt Gertie do?' Then I kind of adopt her party persona. It works every time to help make what I consider to be a dreaded situation fun." It also helps to derail a shyness attack.

Second, remind yourself that being the single person at a couples' event can also be an advantage. Consider: You don't have a partner to worry about so you can arrive when you want, talk to whomever you wish, leave when you please, say whatever. "One of the best things about being single at a couples' event, or any event really, is that my old boyfriend isn't by my side, saying, 'Are you sure you need that piece of cake?' He was a fit-ness buff and was always nag-ging me to lose weight," said Bridget, a newly single Shy who also recently ditched her bathroom scale. There's definitely a freedom in being the single person in a couples' world, if you're willing to find the silver lining and accentuate the positive.

And because you're not doing the couples thing, those who are may find you intriguing and even "adopt" you. "At a wedding reception recently, I encountered an outgoing older couple who made it their business to make sure I met every other single person in the room," said Adrian, a shy engineer in his early thirties. "It was a little embarrassing, but still, they introduced me to tons of women and I even got the number of a 'contender.'" It's true: Couples can serve as social conduits, so don't rule them out.

One-half of a couple can be equally helpful. For example, if you notice a woman sitting alone whose husband is on the dance floor, she may welcome you joining her to talk, no matter which gender you are. She may also end up being a good contact to introduce you to an available someone she knows. A caveat: If you're a woman and you see a married man sitting alone, proceed with caution. Other married women, including his wife, may perceive you as a threat. If the wife reacts, an innocuous moment could become one of self-conscious pain, a sure precursor for prolonged payback.

THE MAP READER IN THE RELATIONSHIP

Another challenging situation for a Shy is asking relationship questions of someone you're dating: Where do you think this is going? Do we agree or do we not agree that we have a future together? Do you love me? Do you love me not? In an apparently blossoming yet undefined relationship, bringing up the subject of the other person's intentions is always difficult because with it comes the possibility of rejection, of having to end a relationship that's pleasant enough or even (to you) going well. But because of their supersensitivity to rejection, to Shys, asking the question is often excruciating. While none of us enjoy discovering we're misreading things or that our love is unrequited, or even that there are problems about which we are unaware, Shys tend to be especially afraid of the "wrong" answer. Of course, it's difficult for anyone to accept a response other than "Yes, of course, we're a couple. Wasn't that assumed?" Even nonshy singles don't accept "no" or even a hesitant response very well. For Shys, however, the possibility of that sort of feedback is their Achilles' heel. In fact, many would rather torture themselves with speculation (and payback) than speak up; there's no more powerful stimuli for triggering the fear of initiation.

"It's exquisitely frustrating," said Janet, a retail salesperson in her early twenties. She had been steadily dating someone for six months whose intentions were elusive. "You wonder, 'Why doesn't he call? How come he's always late? Shouldn't I know more of his friends?'" she said. "Then you think, 'Is it me? That joke I tried to tell the other night? The blouse I wore with the ruffles? Am I too uptight about being prompt? Am I too needy?' The clincher is when his parents are in town. I spend days waiting, then wondering, *Why didn't he invite me over?*" Someone in the group, clearly the voice of experience, chimed in, "And finally, you think, 'Maybe I'm the only one in this relationship.'" "Exactly," Janet said.

As difficult as it is, the big question of "Where are we going?" needs to be asked if it's nagging you. Otherwise, you can spend days, months—and yes, even years—watchfully, resentfully waiting for your partner to show you his hand. And take heart: the spectrum of feedback you may get—from "I don't know where this is going" to "Well, there are some things I've been meaning to talk to you about"—can ultimately improve your relationship. Asking the defining question can help you, as a couple, flesh out issues that need to be aired to get your relationship on a better track.

This is why I encourage you, after asking the question, to openly hear your partner out. Try not to personalize hesitancy and deduce that you're hopelessly inadequate to receive true love, as many of the Shys in my workshops initially do. Such a self-centered "You don't love me" response leaves no room for your partner to brainstorm with you about what fears, inadequacies, and resistances she might have—things that could have nothing to do with you and don't necessarily signal the end of the relationship. Moreover, if there's something she wishes to bring up that bothers her about you or the relationship, your defeated response can thwart the process, or even cause a premature end.

"I used to hate it when my girlfriend informed me that we needed to 'work on our relationship,'" said Larry, a shy bartender in his mid-forties, who was on the receiving end of the "Where is this going?" question. "To me, it sounded like a euphemism for 'There's stuff about you that needs fixing.' We stopped seeing each other because I couldn't take it. Either it's working or it's not." Larry's assessment isn't necessarily correct; most relationships are indeed works in progress.

And unless you can treat whatever relationship feedback your partner gives you as constructive criticism, he may decide to bail out to avoid the emotional fallout. "I'm normally pretty quiet, but when it comes to dealing with the gray areas of boyfriend issues—like why we've been dating for six months and I still haven't seen his apartment—I become a drama queen," said Bethany, a Shy in her mid-twenties who was contemplating dating other people while her on-again/off-again relationship with Kyle sorted itself out. "I'm trying to stay calm and listen to Kyle's subtext, but it's hard because I know I really like him. It's tough to understand why he's so ambivalent." Bethany was frustrated by the limbo she was in, yet she had asked the hard question. "At least now, we're talking about us, which is better than just assuming everything's okay," she said.

Your Big-Question-Asking Action Plan

If you've been dating someone for at least six months and you think it's exclusive but you're not sure, it's fair game to ask: "So, is it safe to say that we're not dating other people?" "How do you feel about us dating just each other?" "Where are you at?" If you've been dating someone exclusively for a year and you think the relationship is solid, bringing up the concept of marriage is a very logical leap, especially if it has never been mentioned before. To get the words out, consider asking about it in a global sort of way: "So, do you think you'll ever get married? Is that something you want for yourself?" Then, take it from there.

Practice asking these all-important questions so you'll be comfortable hearing them coming out of your mouth. Rehearsing protects you from being controlled by the fear of initiation. Brace yourself for a less-than-positive response (just in case) with a lifesaving mantra such as, *If he's not the one, then I deserve to know so I can keep moving.* Having a mantra is a guard against a full-blown assault of stages two and three. Amanda, one of my shy single clients, has this likeable phrase to ease the anticipated sting: "I want to be with someone who wants to be with me. If he doesn't want to be with me, then I don't want to be with him." Amanda's worst fears were confirmed when she confronted Ted. But even though their breakup was very disappointing to her, she was able to start dating again after only a few months of licking her wounds.

Once you bring up the topic, take into account body language and other cues that signal how your partner may be feeling and thinking. If she doesn't call for days after the "Where are we going?" question, she's sending some kind of message. But before you take it as rejection, or portend to truly know what it means, you need to ask her directly: "What's up?" This can also be a tough question to pose. Still, the feedback you get can be useful. If she happens to respond by bringing up issues that perhaps she has been meaning to discuss, hear her out as dispassionately as possible and try to address solutions.

If the stumbling blocks your partner presents are reasonable—maybe she doesn't like it when you're impatient with waiters, chew with your mouth open (who knew?), or answer your call waiting while you're talking to her and spend some time with the other caller—hear her out. You probably didn't realize you did those things or that they bothered her. Fair enough. These are reasonable changes to ask for. If the issues your partner mentions are unreasonable—the fact that your mother's always calling (implication: Your relationship with your mother needs to change); she's allergic to your cat (implication: It's the cat or me); or a physical characteristic, such as you need to lose weight/get in shape/get a nose job—and she can't find a way to live with these things, then perhaps she's not the one for you. Similarly, if she's suggesting that you smoke or drink too much, are too focused on cleanliness, speak too fast, climax too soon— these kinds of issues are hard to change without (probably) a lifetime commitment. "I knew we were in trouble when my boyfriend started complaining about how I kissed," said Sierra, an accountant in her mid-twenties. "One day, he even took his thumb and index finger and pursed my lips together and said, 'There. Your mouth is too open.' Kissing is so basic. We didn't date much longer after that. That pursed kiss was the kiss of death."

Of course, there's always the possibility that the issues or objections your partner brings up are not really about you. Some people have a fear of commitment (FOC), the fear of being controlled or swallowed up in another person's identity. No one is ever quite right for those with FOC, including themselves, because they cannot find

COACH'S CORNER

If you talk yourself out of asking the "Where are we going?" question—or chicken out—consider pouring your heart out, and getting the question on the table, through e-mail. Since you're not face to face, you may get a more honest answer. Plus, you can edit your question until you feel it's phrased just right. A few pointers: Speak from the heart. Aim for directness. And to soften the edges of this question, feel free to use humor, even if this takes real effort on your part.

their own space within a love relationship. The objections your partner raises about "getting serious" can clue you in to whether he has FOC, especially if the objections echo reasons that ended his previous relationships. For example, if he tells you to lose weight or get in better shape, even though he had no complaints up until this defining "Where are we going?" moment, bells should go off—especially if these were the issues he raised with previous girlfriends. FOC is tough to resolve without professional help. But take comfort in the fact that if his demands aren't reasonable, it's not about you; it's about him. He has to deal with his fear of commitment before he can have any serious relationship.

In some cases, it may be too soon to determine where a relationship is going because your partner just doesn't know. If your partner requests more time, you have to decide whether you want to allot it—and how much you want to give. At least you've started a dialogue, which is much better than wasting months, even years. If, after asking "Where are we going?" you're rejected, try my suggestions later in this chapter for easing the pain; likewise, if you find yourself doing the rejecting after posing the big question, look to the next page.

FACING REJECTION

The huge obstacle for Shys is when they're either doing the rejecting or being rejected in a relationship. One of the possibilities in any new dating situation is that it's a potentially poor match. But for some Shys, this potential reality can become so threatening, they may unknowingly bring it on themselves— even when they're in a relationship that's working. When it's over ("Whew!"), you may even feel justified ("I just can't date; I'm no good at it"), but lonely and miserable at the same time. You may also suffer from prolonged payback. ("Nobody is ever going to love me. I'm going to turn out just like my forty-five-year-old cousin who's childless and not married.") Or, conversely, you may resist ending a relationship you no longer enjoy because you don't want to deal with the conflict of saying good-bye, or maybe you lack confidence about maintaining your boundaries if you say it's over. Should the other person disagree with the breakup, you face a potentially ugly situation.

Or perhaps you resist moving on because you empathize so strongly. "I don't want to hurt their feelings," many shy singles have reported in my workshops, always cringing, even when it's the best decision. Samantha was in such a relationship. She had been dating Tom for two years and had been racking up credit card bills on airline tickets (it was a bicoastal relationship). Trouble was, for various reasons, she knew he wasn't the man for her. "But I just can't bring myself to break up with him," she told me repeatedly. "He's such a sweet guy." It was clear that Samantha was identifying with Tom's feelings—to her detriment. By staying in a relationship that needed to end, her pain was escalating as the illusion continued, with Tom occasionally mentioning the prospect of marriage. They were on completely different pages, and Samantha's hesitancy in ending things was creating a real problem. She was frozen in stage two for almost two years. Tom was being set up for an even harder fall, and Samantha's awareness that she was continuing a futureless relationship was making her feel weak and foolish. "I'm such a wimp," she said one evening. Samantha's situation is an example of how a prolonged stage two—overloaded with emotion and completely frozen—becomes a truly debilitating state. The payback that follows this frozen state adds further insult to injury.

Being the Rejecter

The difficulty of saying "No, thank you" to someone who wants the relationship to continue is directly proportional to the amount of self-criticism you heap upon yourself. The more self-critical you are, the less clear you're apt to be about your inten-

COACH'S CORNER

If you must, write a letter, send an e-mail, or use the phone. Depending on how long you were together, a breakup doesn't necessarily have to be done in person, but doing it face-to-face contributes a sense of closure; it's also more humane. While abruptness is cleaner, it can be more traumatic and much more difficult for the other person to recover from; face to face, on the other hand, gives the other person a chance to say goodbye to you. Otherwise, an out-of-the blue, sudden goo-bye may induce in the other person an extreme obsessive reaction in which he is preoccupied with what he did to turn you off.

tions. If you're very self-critical, you may find it almost impossible to tell the other person why you want to end the relationship for fear that anything you say will sound like criticism rather than a statement of what's best for you.

If you're the one who wants to end the relationship, try thinking that the sooner you say goodbye, the faster he can find somebody else who is more suited to him. You're actually setting both of you free to find a more mutually satisfying relationship. Even though breakups can be agonizing, it's not fair to hold on to someone because you don't have the guts to end it. And if you consider the "don't do unto others" rule, you wouldn't want to be bound in a relationship that's not working longer than you should be either, would you?

Your Rejector Action Plan

To make doing the deed as easy as possible, create a breakup line you're comfortable with that's simple to remember, repeatable, and doesn't sound attacking. Try something like: "After all this time we've spent together, I just don't think we have that special something couples need to make it for the long run." Chances are, sensing your vulnerability, your partner may object and even try to talk you out of breaking up with him. When that happens, simply restate your case: "I'm sorry. I don't want to hurt you. But I don't think we have that special something couples need to make it for the long run." If you add, "I don't want to waste your time, or mine for that matter," you'll appear stronger. Keep repeating yourself if you need to, then exit the situation as quickly as possible. Having a set speech that you repeat softly, but consistently, can help you with the fear of initiation and freezing or flooding. Knowing what you are going to say, you won't be overwhelmed with so many options that nothing emerges, nor will spill out more than you want to say. Your breakup line can also help to thwart payback, because you minimize the unplanned, which can trigger subsequent self-criticism.

In case your breakup line doesn't having the desired effect, have a backup "insurance policy" at the ready. Tell your former lover that there's no possibility for another chance because you're now sure that you must find someone who is something that this person is not—your religion, not divorced, a local (you know she can never leave her hometown to move to yours), your race, or any other immutable quality that your former lover can never attain. Like your breakup line, this statement requires repeated practice. In the end, though, it is the kindest approach you can take, because it ultimately leaves no room for false hope.

Another preparation strategy involves role-playing with a trusted friend. Ask your friend to be as difficult as possible. Go over scenarios that will have the former lover resisting the goodbye. Then, when the real scene happens, it'll likely be easier than the imagined ones. You'll walk away feeling more satisfied with the outcome, which is the best strategy for warding off payback.

Getting Rejected

Vulnerable Shys tend to suffer greatly from the pain of rejection; again, self-criticism looms large. The more self-critical you are, the less you'll be able to tolerate comments you perceive as negative from your partner. Not surprisingly, therefore, the end of a relationship that wasn't your decision can be tough.

As I discussed in chapter five, you may be hardwired for self-blame as a result of your formative years. Often, the severest self-critics had a childhood in which there was so much chaos or other diversions in the family that the quiet child who made no fuss was ignored and, as a result, felt invisible. Or perhaps the child grew up in an authoritarian home environment where an iron rule was imposed on the household by at least one of the caregivers. Either of these situations can cause a child to become highly self-critical as an adult. Both invisibility and abundant disapproval become equated with not being good enough because a person learns to vigilantly self-monitor his or her actions to keep the peace (and avoid harm).

Grace, a divorced realtor in her early forties who thought she had finally found a man who would successfully end her dating career, came from such a household. Her father ruled the house by fear. "If you cried because you were upset, he'd say, 'Quit crying or I'll give you something to cry about.' My father made us all feel unsafe around him. I steered clear and always tried to stay on his good side." Grace came to my workshop because she had just been "unceremoniously dumped." The surprise breakup was enough to rock what little confidence she had. "If only I had worn sexier lingerie, cooked dinner for him more often, tried to be more athletic. . . . " Her list trailed on. Grace was kitchen-sinking it, which is a common reaction, and it was magnifying her pain. She blamed herself for the breakup, even though she had given the relationship her all. (If this sounds like payback, that's because it is. Nothing is as certain to trigger it as a sudden goodbye.) "Maybe I wasn't worthy of his love. And maybe I'm not good enough for anyone else's either," Grace concluded. At that moment she couldn't imagine there'd be others who might be a better match for her than "Mr. Wonderful." During the first blush of disappointment, Grace couldn't put this rejection in perspective. But since then, she's been working with the tips that follow to help her see "no" in a new light.

Your Rejectee Action Plan

Reframe rejection as a blessing in disguise. Ask yourself: *What do I gain by not having this person in my life? What adjustments was I making to accommodate her idiosyncrasies? What do I no longer have to put up with that I disliked while we were together? What freedoms did I forego to meet him more than halfway?* Consider writing your answers in your journal or diary, which can serve as a record for identifying patterns both in yourself and in those dates that didn't work out. The more you discover about what *isn't* a good match, the better you can develop your own assessment about what kind of person *is.*

Rather than wallow in payback, take time to reflect and ask yourself insight-provoking questions, such as: "What did I learn from this experience? What am I going to do differently next time?" If you're not sure, ask others who knew you as a couple. (If you like, write your answers in a journal for future reference.) You may not agree with all of the opinions of your former lover and friends, but some of the comments might be helpful for future relationships. Like your successes, relationships that didn't go well can be equally valuable—if only to teach you what to avoid.

When Marnie, a shy choreographer in her mid-thirties, thought about these questions, she realized that since she was no longer with Jeff—someone she had dated for six months who ended their relationship because he said he needed to spend more time trying to make partner at his law firm—she was free to choose a mate who wouldn't put her second fiddle to his work. "Now I have my radar on. No workaholics for me!" she said proudly. Similarly, Conrad, a computer consultant in his late twenties, realized that he'd save a lot of money on phone bills after his long-distance girlfriend of three years called it quits (over the phone, of course). "From now on," he said, "I'm only going to date women who live in my city. It's not just the phone bills. Commuter relationships

COACH'S CORNER

The shy tend to regard failure as something they caused and success as just luck or chance. Avoid this mistake. It's unproductive and energy draining.

are brutal. I want someone I can see a couple of times a week, not once a month."

Next, study the part of the relationship that worked or parts of other relationships in the past, even platonic ones, that worked. What did you bring to the partnership that made it satisfying for you as well as the other person? Write your answers in your journal or diary.

Finally, realize that each person walking away from a relationship is experiencing a loss. Allow yourself to grieve. You need comforting. And while you're at it, be kind to yourself and take some time to make yourself feel better. It doesn't have to be a day at the spa or a night on the town (or the prowl), although it could be. Perhaps it's a good time to take a vacation to somewhere completely unlike where you live. As you rack up frequent flier miles, you'll gain emotional distance and perhaps a healthier perspective for a fresh start when you return.

DOWNSIZING YOUR SELF-CONSCIOUSNESS

Now that you've tackled the tough issue you were facing, how do you manage the huge case of self-consciousness that inevitably follows? How do you work, step by step, to avoid a shyness attack? First, identify the situations, or specific aspects of situations, that activate your fearfulness. Is it the cocktail hour at the wedding that you find the most difficult? Is it how you phrase the "Where are we going?" question so that you don't sound desperate? Is it the anticipated several minutes after you break up with your boyfriend you're dreading the most, the time when you know he'll look particularly sad or, worse, grovel? The key is to accept this difficult moment and prepare for it. The more aware you are, the less power your sensitive and self-conscious nature will acquire in the moment. Your insight and honesty will help you set a smoother course. For example, if your pattern has been to avoid ending unfulfilling relationships, the next time you meet a potential partner, you'll be primed to remind yourself: *In the past, I've hung on too long in relationships I wanted to end, because I told myself I didn't want to hurt the other person. I'm not going to do that anymore. Waiting makes it worse, and it's emotionally draining not to honor my own opinion about what is best for me. This time, I'm going to set the person free if I find out we're not well-matched.*

Once you acknowledge your fearfulness and prepare for it, adopt a "can-do" attitude and acknowledge that you do have options in any of these emotionally seismic situations. Instead of passively waiting to react to someone else's initiative if, for example, you're the lone ranger at a party, you could identify the positive in this image (you're unencumbered—and by the way, the real Lone Ranger was a hero) and ask yourself what advantages your singleness offers that coupled people don't share. Then act accordingly. You could flirt with the waiter, dance with a variety of people (even the coupled ones, if you are sure their partners don't mind), and make the rounds through the room without worrying about whom you're not paying attention to or getting into trouble with a partner. If you're concerned about the future with your partner or merely want to establish the current reality, you have options there, as well: You could continue to wait, hoping something will come to light, or you could gently broach the subject and give yourself self-esteem-boosting credit for being proactive. If you're getting the boot in a relationship or doing the booting, envisioning it as setting the other person free or being freed yourself can make the transition easier.

Recognizing your choices, such as how you elect to view the situation that you previously experienced as negative or harsh, can help you remain in control rather than feel victimized by your circumstances. This is true even if you're blindsided by a turn of events, like your partner saying he really doesn't see you in his future. Though it might not be the answer you hoped to hear, his feelings are out, and you're not hovering in agonizing uncertainty. Even in this situation, you could compose a thank-you note to him for not wasting your time. (You don't have to send it.)

Finally, as always, you need to become your own change agent and develop an on-the-spot action plan that can help you initiate the small steps that build an increasing sense of accomplishment and generate momentum. Start by asking yourself, *How do I want to handle this particular situation?* Then give yourself what I call a conscious homework assignment that can help you solve the problem during the event or encounter. Sound easier to think about than do? Not if you set your mind to it. When the going gets tough, the tough (that would be you) employ survival strategies, such as those I suggest in this chapter for strengthening yourself in the three challenging situations we've been discussing.

If payback gives you a call after you encounter confidence-threatening experiences (and it's bound to), refer to chapter five to quell your inner critic. By now, you may have a favorite payback tactic (or two) that works reliably for you. Now is the perfect time to put it into play. If not, keep experimenting with the various payback-squelching options I suggest, starting on page 92, until you have an arsenal at your disposal to fend off the fray.

WHAT'S YOUR COURAGE SCORE?

We complete this chapter with your courage score. On a scale of 1 to 10, with 1 being the courage of a kitten (you buried your nose in a magazine at a couples' cocktail party), and 10 the courage of a lion (you finally ended a relationship with which you were dissatisfied), rate your difficult situation courage score.

Take a situation that was very uncomfortable for you and score yourself. Circle your score below.

1 1.5 2 2.5 3 3.5 4 4.5 5 5.5 6 6.5 7 7.5 8 8.5 9 9.5 10

You may wish to write your score in the space that follows: _____

Then consider a situation that is coming up in the future. How courageous do you feel today about the event that is about to happen? Circle your score below.

1 1.5 2 2.5 3 3.5 4 4.5 5 5.5 6 6.5 7 7.5 8 8.5 9 9.5 10

You may wish to write your score in the space that follows: _____

If your courage score is still more kitten than lion, ask yourself what you can incorporate from your action plans to increase your score just half a courage-building point. For example, give yourself half a point if you actively plan how you'll ask the "Where are we going?" question, which is useful even if you don't go through with it on that particular day or at that time. At least you'll have a plan on the back burner. Remember, as long as you live, breathe, and take chances, courage-challenging situations, such as those in this chapter, will occasionally find you, but they can only derail your self-confidence if you're caught off guard, unprotected, and unprepared to deal with them. Confidence comes from being prepared.

"It is easy to be brave from a safe distance."

—Aesop

{NINE}

WHEN YOU'RE SHY AROUND
THOSE YOU KNOW

SYLVIA MET DANIEL AT A CLUB MED GETAWAY. They walked the beach for hours, spent ages in each other's rooms. Life had finally handed them a great gift. Then they returned to reality in New York City. Sylvia seemed increasingly distant and unavailable. "She's not the same woman I met on the beach. I feel like I've been duped," said Daniel. But Sylvia wasn't snubbing him or a fraud; she fit into a group of Shys who become shy when they get closer to someone.

For these Shys, the toughest part of dating isn't making small talk at cocktail parties or the self-revelatory, getting-to-know-you Saturday nights out; it's the getting-to-know-you-better weeks, when, as a couple, they spend more time one on one. While intimacy—and I don't necessarily mean sex (more on that later)—can be challenging enough even for the most outgoing of us, for those who are shy around people they know, it can be terrifying. Indeed, intimacy is fertile ground for a shyness attack.

There are two sorts of intimacy shyness—one is verbal, the other sexual. (Some people are shy in both arenas and experi-

ence an attack differently in each.) Those who are shy in conversation may feel comfortable expressing themselves with their
bodies and are usually not shy in bed. Others, who may be quite
at ease verbally, may feel uncomfortable with physical touching,
kissing, caresses, or nudity. Both types of shyness appear once
you've already broken the ice and you're well on your way to
getting to know someone. You may even be an established
couple.

WHEN YOU'RE VERBALLY SHY

Feeling too exposed and self-conscious, those who become
shy around people they know may maintain a distance and, as a
result, stifle an opportunity to deepen a relationship. Verbal shyness tends to emerge as they spend more time with someone.
"At around the third date with a man I'm really interested in, I
always start feeling really self-conscious and worry that I'll say
the wrong thing or somehow 'blow it,'" said Pearl, a thirty-eight-
year-old computer programmer. "Then I start pulling back to
protect myself and canceling dates. Getting past that third-date
milestone would be a real breakthrough for me."

Kayla, another workshop participant, nodded. "The more I realize I like someone and our dates 'count,' the more careful and
withdrawn I become," she said. "With each date, I seem to say less
and less, especially if I'm really interested. I nod a lot and keep my
opinions to myself. Sometimes I even say to myself during a third
or fourth date, 'You're *not* this shy, silent woman,' but I clam up.
I'm too shy to talk about myself."

As if your suffering weren't enough, when you're verbally shy
around someone you know, as Pearl and Kayla are, you're often
misunderstood. Your dates may interpret your reactions (or lack
thereof) as disinterest, coldness, meanness, lack of intelligence,
self-centeredness, or even depression. Yet, on the contrary, you
want to get to know your date better, not scare him away. But
because you're verbally shy, you have trouble stepping out of it

to level with him, so your date remains in the dark, free to misinterpret.

Verbal shyness can be the fear of conflict when delivering bad news ("I think we should see other people") or dealing with certain aspects of your relationship. It may feel impossible for you to have "the talk," whatever talk it is you're facing. Marianne, a shy biotechnology researcher in her early thirties, for example, met Russell, an extroverted man who had a lot of the qualities she was looking for. "He is the first man who is really an equal," she said. "He's also funny and he can talk about anything." But Russell was also controlling, especially in the kitchen. Cooking was a hobby Marianne shared with him, and after six months of dating, trouble was brewing. "He's always telling me what knife

WHEN THE FEAR OF EMOTIONAL INTIMACY IS REALLY THE FEAR OF COMMITMENT

As I touched upon in chapter eight, sometimes discomfort with getting close to another person—whether it's in the living room or in the bedroom—can be confused with the near-apocryphal fear of commitment (FOC). Many of my workshop participants worry they have FOC, but they discover that discomfort with intimacy is really their problem. Here's the difference: Usually a person with a resistance to commitment finds a twosome too confining. Consciously or subconsciously, he or she may believe there's always another, perhaps more desirable, conquest right around the corner. How can she trust both herself and her partner that this choice is the best she can make? He may imagine that his friends or relatives will disapprove of his choice. Everyone must secretly think he can do better, and he agrees.

FOC is usually a deep distrust of one's own judgment, which is often the result of being raised by overbearing caretakers who have usurped their child's inalienable right to make his or her own decisions. The extreme is self-distrust, which may develop when a child is compelled to fend for himself before he is actually preto use and how to do certain cooking techniques. I don't need his 'help,' as he puts it. I've been cooking myself for years," she said. Marianne worried that her boyfriend's controlling nature would spread to other parts of their relationship and eventually drive her over the edge.

To break the pattern, Marianne needed to tell Russell when his habits made her angry, a task she found impossible due to her shyness. "I want to tell him, 'Cut it out. You're taking all the fun out of cooking together,' but somehow I can't," she said. She worried that if she tried to say her piece, he could argue, or not have the patience to let her fully express herself. Other Shys in similar confrontational circumstances have reported being worried the other person will misunderstand what they want to say,

---

pared. Later in life, he may doubt his ability to get his choices "right."

In contrast, fear of emotional intimacy implies fear of being overwhelmed by a love interest, yet craving a special person and abhorring loneliness. In this case, you need to feel safe before revealing parts of yourself. You require time to know whether you truly like and trust your partner, if the relationship is going anywhere, and whether you want it to. As the questions are answered, safety follows, although feeling "safe" may take a little time to achieve.

If you're hesitant to sleep with or even kiss someone you've just met and perhaps have been talking to for a couple of hours, that doesn't necessarily mean fear of intimacy. It could mean that you have a point of view about where and when you choose to express your sexuality. Conversely, if you're able to have sex with someone relatively new, that doesn't mean you *don't* have a fear of emotional intimacy. Some people rush into a sexual encounter to avoid conversation (emotional intimacy). In this case, sex can actually keep the relationship from developing, and unless the couple breaks the pattern, it may interfere with getting to know each other on other levels.

feel insulted, or tell them they're crazy. "I'll probably end up even more frustrated," Marianne concluded. After a lengthy discussion with the group, she decided to break her pattern of not speaking up by calmly and good-naturedly calling him on it each time an incident occurred. "Uh, there you go again, being the head chef," one workshop participant suggested, a phrase which Marianne resolved to try. "We're not cured, but he's much more aware of what angers me, and I'm much more able to laugh during our cooking projects," she told the group several weeks later.

Managing Verbal Shyness

To help with verbal shyness, review my suggestions for managing stage two of a shyness attack, starting on page 65. What worked for you in managing circuit overload around strangers may also help you overcome any verbal intimacy issues that surface once you're in a deepening relationship. Here are some other strategies to try.

- **Confess.** When you find yourself verbally shy, for example, on your third or fourth date, tell her. By saying, "You know, I might not have seemed this way in the beginning, but I'm actually kind of shy," you help that person understand that your silence or demureness isn't about her. At the very least, telling someone you really like (or think you may even be falling in love with) that you're too shy to say too much heads off the fear of initiation. Even if you can't say more than that, at least you've helped your date avoid misinterpreting your silence to mean you find her boring or that you're somehow angry with her.

- **Instruct your date.** You could mention what your date might do when you retreat into yourself by saying: "If I'm too quiet, go ahead and bring up a topic or ask me a question." This approach can even work if you have trouble saying "I love you" or reciprocating it in a conversation (assuming you truly feel that way). For example, you could tell your partner that when you say "me, too" you really mean it, but it's just difficult for you to say "I love you" back (or even to initiate those magic words).

- **Practice compassion.** Be sensitive to the other person's feelings of rejection and reassure him that you do notice him, regardless of whether you speak. To help gather your courage, try empathizing; your shyness may make him feel invisible, and you know how painful that is.

Your Verbal Intimacy Action Plan

Which strategies will you attempt to ward off encroaching verbal shyness around those you know? Jot down some thoughts in the space that follows.

_____

_____

_____

_____

_____

_____

_____

To break down your action plan into small, more manageable steps, focus on one aspect of your verbal shyness you'd like to conquer. Imagine a verbally intimate situation, such as a fourth or fifth date or trying to tell your mate you love her, and complete the statement below. Remember, writing it down makes it real and more committed to memory. Consider photocopying this page for easy reference.

The next time I find myself in a verbally intimate situation, I'd like to try to manage my shyness by:

_____

_____

———————————————————

———————————————————

———————————————————

———————————————————

———————————————————

———————————————————

WHEN YOU'RE SEXUALLY SHY

One aspect of intimate shyness involves sexuality. In the first stage of a shyness attack, it's the fear of initiating making love. Those who are sexually shy may be reluctant to get fully undressed unless the lights are out. It's understandable; after all, with sex, you're potentially vulnerable in every word, sigh, movement, and sensation from the shedding of clothes to the expression of feelings to the closeness of skin on skin. Embarrassed by their own sexuality or afraid of the act itself, Shys may make themselves appear unreceptive. "I literally jumped when Jerry tried to touch me," said Corinne, a twenty-eight-year-old physical therapist, who had been dating Jerry for four months. "Then I gathered my things and fled his apartment. I claimed I was exhausted from work."

In the second stage of a shyness attack, the sexually shy may feel too paralyzed to utter a sound. Or, they may chatter. I know many shy singles who can override their initial fear of verbal intimacy during their first several dates, only to find themselves talking up a storm at the prospect of sex. For them, words are their greatest delay tactic. They subconsciously use the flooding aspect of stage two as a form of self-protection: 'If I just keep talking . . . maybe "it" won't happen and I won't have to be exposed or vulnerable or threatened.'

If your sexual style is highly verbal but you can detect that all this chatter doesn't bring you and your lover closer, it's possible that you're using a defense mechanism to protect yourself from a primal fear of losing control. The word *primal* is quite intentional. As children, we were all at the beck and call of grownups, who decided when our basic needs would be met. If you had parents who were insensitive to your discomfort at being completely under their grip, you may have developed an intense aversion to the necessity of surrender, which can carry over and interfere with the joy of submission as a willing adult. Shys who fall into this category believe it's better to keep talking and thereby cling to their emotional clothes. Ironically, shy obsessive talkers often find relief when they and their partner do take off their clothes because both naked people are vulnerable, and thus, on an equal playing field.

On the other hand, perhaps you'd *like* to talk more during sex. Maybe you think you're too quiet. If so, perhaps your intimacy style is ruled by self-consciousness. When this self-absorption occurs in the sexual arena, you're more in bed with yourself than with your partner. If you become overly focused on your performance, the fallout can include lack of erection and/or premature ejaculation, the inability to have an orgasm, and a feeling of emptiness and loneliness for both people. If your nonshy partner ventures to give feedback about something he would like or even dislikes, beware of your self-consciousness increasing. Without realizing it, you may shoot the messenger and blame him for any sexual frustrations you may have. This brings us to . . .

What happens post-encounter. During the third stage of a shyness attack, the sexually shy may brutally criticize their performance after an intimate encounter. Joan, a fifty-something, divorced jazz singer, agonized for days about an intimate encounter gone bad. After a few dates with a particularly "interesting" man, she invited him up to her apartment. She was warm and seductive. "Things were moving along nicely until he said, 'I want to please you,'" Joan explained. Gulp. That comment was the kiss of intimate death. "I began to stammer that I hardly knew him," Joan said, which wasn't exactly true. After all, "I felt comfortable enough to invite him up to my apartment. Obviously, I was open to the possibility that things might lead to sex," she said. Mr. Interesting suggested just cuddling in the bedroom "so we could get comfortable with each other." Joan replied that she didn't have that in mind at all. He left soon after and hadn't called by the time Joan came to see me. She proceeded to review everything she said and did the night of the date and even before. "I really like him, so I'm driving myself crazy," she confessed. She was completely uncertain of the next step. Should she call him? Wait and hope for him to call her?

Was Joan second-guessing her refusal, wavering on her boundaries about having sex too soon in a new relationship? More likely, her payback was connected to her experience of stage two and the one-sided nature of Mr. Interesting's suggestion. Joan surmised, "When he said he wanted to please me, I suddenly felt under so much pressure to perform, to have to act like he was pleasing me. That's when I got scared." Still, Joan didn't want to throw away this otherwise perfectly good start of a relationship, so she decided to call Mr. Interesting and invite him over for dinner. It was possible they could recover from this experience by approaching it from a different angle, yet the invitation meant that Joan had to face her own fears that he might not want to see her again. "If I invite him for dinner, he could reject me head-on," she said. "But that's okay. If it's going to happen, I want to know sooner rather than later." Joan had intelligently decided to try to manage her intimate shyness problem one step at a time.

When you're like Joan, your discomfort with physical exposure can hold you back during an encounter. And yet, who can blame you? For many, getting physically naked makes them emotionally naked as well. And sometimes, the conditions just aren't right. Maybe it's too soon in a relationship. Maybe your partner's physical chemistry, her views on family or politics, or her handling of her work life don't mesh with your value system and you can't or don't want to take it another step—not yet anyway. Maybe the way he expresses his desires turns you off, as in Joan's case.

Feeling shy about sex with someone you've come to know quite well may reflect your past experiences as well as your current history as part of this couple. For example, if you're shy and you have a tendency to keep long-term, ongoing secrets from your partner—who might have offended, confused, or frightened you—the sex will suffer, as will other passions. In time, you'll begin to resent your partner in seemingly unrelated ways for the unspoken business between you. Or, in trying to keep the secret, you'll become moody, and one day, you may blurt it out in a manner that fulfills your prediction—that the person on the receiving end will get angry and possibly leave for good. Diane, a forty-four-year-old lawyer, had a secret she was keeping from Ron. "If I tell Ron that I know he called me while he was still dating Caroline (which, to be honest, offended me), he may get angry at me for having kept this to myself for the last six months. He might think, 'What else does she find offensive that she hasn't told me?' But keeping this to myself is getting in the way in the bedroom." Diane did blurt out the secret in a tense moment, and, Ron, out of embarrassment, did get angry and considered leaving. But after some tears and a week of the silent treatment, Ron began to understand that Diane's feelings of playing second fiddle to Caroline were more related to something from her past and less that he called her as a backup. Diane came to understand that after Ron met her, he no longer felt the same way towards Caroline. They each made a mental note to check in so that secrets wouldn't fester and eventually erode their togetherness. Now they're closer than ever.

Understanding Sexual Shyness

As you can see, sexual shyness is very complex. But viewing the fear of sexual intimacy through the lens of knowledge can help you accept that a sex life is often affected by many other considerations. And with knowledge, you can begin to have hope. As you become more aware of what's going on between you and your partner, the less awkward you'll feel. To help you understand why you may be sexually shy, consider the following list of possible reasons. As you'll notice, many of the phrases appear to have nothing to do with the physical aspects of sex or intimacy; they're more emotional in nature. I've included them here because it's vital not to disconnect the sexual side of ourselves from our spiritual/emotional nature. Maintaining a dual awareness of your physical sensations and your sensitivities can help you bridge the gap. Check the box next to anything below you feel applies to you.

☐ 1. I have a fear of the unexpected.

☐ 2. I have an overwhelming desire to please.

☐ 3. I often anticipate that my partner won't do what I like and I'll be too inhibited to give feedback.

☐ 4. I won't do what my partner likes, and I can't tolerate feedback.

☐ 5. An authority figure from my past warned me against sexual behavior.

☐ 6. I can't imagine I'd be desired "that way."

☐ 7. In an early sexual encounter, I was told certain things about my performance, and they hurt. Now, I hesitate to make a move when it comes to sex.

☐ 8. I'm not sure what to do in this role because I've had little experience.

☐ 9. I don't think I'm sexy; even if my partner tells me I am, I don't believe him.

☐ 10. Sex talk in bed embarrasses me.

Now look over your checked statements and reflect on past and present encounters in which the physical was involved. When did your self-consciousness emerge, and how did it manifest itself? Is there a consistent pattern with nearly every non-platonic relationship you've been in? Write your answers in the space below.

_____

_____

_____

_____

_____

_____

_____

_____

Review your answers above, and consider when the fear of sexual intimacy arises. Complete the following statement.

The fear of sexual intimacy usually affects me when:

_____

_____

_____

_____

_____

_____

_____

Facing the Fear of Initiation in the Bedroom

Among the shy singles in my workshops, one of the biggest roadblocks to satisfying sex is getting started. They tell me that reaching out for their lover can feel like they're leaping off a cliff because they fear rejection. So, often, they wait for clear signals from their partner—or do nothing. When you become paralyzed in a sexual encounter, it's easy for your partner to misinterpret what's actually occurring. She may think you don't find her appealing and then feel angry, cheated, rejected, dejected, or frustrated.

You may also feel frustrated and turn that back on yourself. You may think there's something wrong with you or become angry with your partner for not understanding your plight. "Why can't I just make the first move?" said Kyle, a shy investment banker in his late twenties who was in the midst of a relationship with a more experienced woman. His voice betrayed how disappointed he was in himself.

Luckily, there's help. On the following pages are some suggestions for facilitating sensual and loving initiations when a shyness attack threatens to derail your desire. If you find that you can speak to your partner out of bed but feel inhibited once you

HOW YOUR PAST INFLUENCES YOUR DATING PRESENT

If you're having trouble "surrendering" in sex, no matter what you try, there may be more layers to it than mere shyness. Sometimes besides the two people in bed, there's a third, invisible "presence." This ephemeral force, called an introject, could be the image or "voice" of your partner's mother, your father, grandparents, your kids or boss, your siblings, or your best friends—anyone from your past or present who powerfully impacts your conscious and unconscious thoughts, influencing how you relate to your partner, especially in an intimate context. These "love triangles" involve one or more individuals, past or present, who have been key in the formation of your sense of self.

Triangulating—the term for being unable to keep a destructive introject out of a twosome—is, in most cases, a death knoll to a positive sexual or emotional experience because it allows anxiety and other old feelings to overpower the couple. And, conveniently, your partner can become a target for what's not working, when are about to begin "the act," here are a few hints below that have worked for some shy singles I know.

- **Name it.** Sound familiar? I've discussed this strategy in previous chapters, and it applies to physical intimacy as well. When you're in bed with your partner, for example, you might find that you freeze up and/or suddenly don't know what to do. Or you might start thinking obsessive thoughts about what your partner should be doing differently, or even start thinking about something completely removed, like your job. You may have discovered by now that admitting—either to yourself or out loud—that you're experiencing the fear of initiation is empowering. Try saying to yourself *I'm feeling shy, and I don't know what to do or say.* As I've suggested in previous chapters, by doing so, you'll develop an "observing ego" that can help you be present in the moment and break through your inhibition.

what's really wrong is that you're overattached through anger or other (even positive) emotions to someone else.

If this sounds familiar, you need to release yourself from the grip of your own history. Trace your current emotions to similar ones you had with significant others in your past. By making the unconscious influences conscious, you'll be able to choose how you want to react in certain situations rather than be driven by unknown forces.

It can be difficult to make connections between your past and your present emotions and reactions by yourself. You might want to see a therapist or consult a trusted friend, clergy member, teacher, or relative if you suspect that emotional baggage from your past is haunting your future, or if you simply don't know why you're feeling a certain way. It's important to tackle this now. The fear of rejection from your mate and an inability to reach out and express intimate feelings can keep you from achieving an intimate life, in and out of the bedroom.

- **Try saying "Hi. It's me."** Say a word or two to your lover to break the ice before you begin to embrace, instead of going through the motions in silence. Her response, even if it's just a simple "hi" back, can help you feel more at ease and connected. If you want more than that, explain that you need to talk a little or share a laugh, or enjoy some music together, so that you feel more sexually relaxed and secure. (A back rub might do the trick.) But every couple is different. Experiment to find out what works for you.

- **Be honest about your shyness.** When you're not in bed—perhaps you're walking in the park or having a quiet dinner together—and you're not as shy, talk about it. You might say something like, "I know I have trouble telling you when I want to make love and even letting myself go when I'm in the mood. It's because I feel scared." Talk about sex when there isn't any possibility of it. When you do, you'll create a safer listening environment, and your partner won't think you're trying to put him off. During your talk, be as specific as you can about what disturbs you. It will build his understanding of you and diminish his own thoughts of personal rejection.

- **Say thank you.** Shyness sufferers are often grateful when their partner lovingly initiates. If this is true for you, say so. "You can't imagine how thrilled I am when you reach for me!" is something you could say when you're not in the bedroom (for example, over coffee and the paper the next morning) to let your partner know that that's what you need to plunge through your self-consciousness.

- **Clue each other in.** If your partner is shy as well, agree on a signal system that sex may be in the offing, such as when you hand your lover a whisky sour at a party that night, it means you're considering sex that evening. If he hangs your teddy on the doorknob, he's thinking about wanting to make love. If you wear a certain nightgown or he plays a certain CD, intimate touching could be the next step. The point is to find gently undemanding ways to convey "I think I'm in the mood. How about it?" But have a mutual agreement that it can go either way, that the whisky sour or the hanging teddy, for example, carries with it only the suggestion of sexual intimacy, not an out-and-out demand. If you're not in the mood, agree that turning away in bed isn't a rejection—you just don't feel like it at the time.

COACH'S CORNER

Contrary to popular belief, the majority of good lovers don't just get there because they instinctively know how to please. Their partners verbally and/or nonverbally taught them how to respond. They, in turn, listened and absorbed. For every couple, good sex is learned by doing. And no matter how much you know about yourself or others, each lover presents his own sexual map. It always takes time to learn to read each other's ever-evolving signals.

Here are several more tips that will aid you in dipping into this sweet nectar of life.

1. Be as accepting of your sexual self-consciousness as you would if your partner were the shy one in bed.

2. Find humor in the bedroom. Tell yourself, *This is fun—not a test of my self-worth.*

3. Think of sex as a journey, not a destination. Orgasm is not the only aspect of sex that makes the whole experience worthwhile. In fact, in Tantrism, the goal is to hold off for as long as possible—to enjoy the experience and keep the end in the far-off distance; orgasm is less desirable than the process.

4. Allow small changes. For example, if you rigidly cling to the bedroom, try having sex in the living room.

5. Give yourself as much time as you need to feel secure and familiar with your partner. In fact, the more time you give yourself to get comfortable, the more you're using your time on earth well.

Managing Sexual Shyness: Be Safe

This is not about the barrier methods of contraception. No matter what your sexual style or how shy you are when it comes to sex, you'll need to feel safe in the relationship; emotional security is the preeminent environment for satisfying sex. A feeling of "everything is all right here" is the greatest gift lovers can offer each other so that the delicious experience of surrender is possible. In fact, to have a successful love relationship, both in and out of bed, you must be willing to both create and receive this feeling of physical and emotional safety. Each of us have symbolic actions that can make us feel secure or insecure. For example, one person may feel that a nightgown left on the bed is a nonpushy invitation for sex, while the other person could feel threatened by this gesture—depending on her or his history.

If you're at a stage in your relationship when getting physical is the natural next step, comfort with your partner helps ward off a shyness attack. For some, security in a relationship may mean feeling certain that you're in an exclusive partnership; or security may come from knowing that your partner truly cares for you, that you're more important than other people or other aspects of his life, even his work. If you don't feel secure (according to your own definition or barometer of what it is), you may want to postpone getting physical until you do.

Meredith, an assistant book editor in her late twenties, knew firsthand what it was like to try to have a physical relationship with someone she didn't really trust. She fell in love with Gerald, "a charming property manager with brown hair and dreamy blue eyes," at first sight. But after they started dating, a troubling pattern emerged. Gerald never called when he said he would and would disappear for days, not returning Meredith's calls, always saying he had been swamped at work. "I didn't buy it. Something was up," Meredith said. Still, when Gerald did

HANDLING UNWANTED SEXUAL ADVANCES

Regardless of whether you're shy in bed, the thwarting of an un-wanted sexual advance can be a slippery slope to navigate. Both male and female Shys may be afraid of causing any conflict and rejection that's sure to follow. What's a Shy to do?

"Just say no" isn't just an anti-drug slogan from the eighties. Say "no" firmly and repeat it again as you edge your way out of the apartment, the cab, the party, the bedroom. There's no need to ex-plain why you're saying no. Whether it's a personal boundaries issue or the fact that you're simply not interested, it's your right to refuse. If you decide you want further contact, arrange for a meeting in public where you can explain why you're not interested in sex at this time; then, if he feels rejected or misunderstood, you can listen to his side. When both of you honestly air your feelings, you increase your chances for closeness and subsequent con-sensual sex—when the timing is right.

call, Meredith always agreed to go out with him, rationalizing that he was the kind of man who needed plenty of "space." Their relationship got physical on their third date. In bed, "things are okay," Meredith said, with an anguished look on her face, not wanting to describe in too much detail what exactly was going on. "But the trouble is, I just don't know where I stand with Gerald. Am I his girlfriend? Is he seeing other people? I think I'm a little scared of him." She had reason to be because, in her mind, Gerald held all the cards. Therefore, he didn't appear safe.

As Meredith surmised, he wasn't giving her any reason to feel safe. She decided to curtail the sexual part of their rela-tionship and find out from Gerald what she meant to him. "Maybe he isn't such a great catch after all," she said. After agreeing to sit down and discuss their relationship, Gerald ad-mitted that Meredith was moving faster towards commitment than he was. He had just gone through a painful divorce and didn't want to rush into anything. After he explained and she understood, they started again and Meredith was happier to go slower this time.

Minimizing Payback

If you're prone to payback, a sexually intimate relationship could trigger those familiar obsessive, self-annihilating thoughts of vulnerability. To avoid damaging self-criticism, review the tips in chapter five, starting on page 92. In general, feeling safe first will help to minimize an onslaught. So will appreciating that you're not alone. Sex is emotional for all of us—not only for the shy. Sexual encounters demand a leap into an openness that is a challenge for everyone at times. If you start to reflect on an awkward moment during an intimate encounter, remind yourself that it takes just one person, you, to perceive the moment as anything other than blissful. Change your perspective and enjoy the moment.

Communication is a hallmark of good sex. Still, if you're at a point in your relationship where you feel comfortable telling your partner what you like him to do (or do differently) in the bedroom, take heed. Because sex is so personal, he could read between the lines, hearing "you're an oaf" or "I hate it when you . . . " To make this important conversation easier—and to minimize the chance that payback will pay you a visit—I suggest telling your partner what pleases you when you make love before offering a truth about what could make you feel even better. You might try, for example, "I really loved it when you touched me so firmly. Could you do that more?" The goal is to inform, not criticize.

You can model what "informed" looks like by asking for suggestions on what he may enjoy. When you're in the listener's seat, especially if your partner is blunt in how he tells you what he wants, repeat to yourself, "He's telling me what makes *him* feel good, not that I'm bad at sex," or "I'm fine. I just need to learn what *she* likes or what makes *her* feel excited." Remember, both of you have the right not to comply, and all couples' tastes and inclinations may change over time into alternative ways of being with each other, depending on life circumstances.

Your Sexual Intimacy Action Plan

Now review the general guidelines for managing the fear of sexual intimacy throughout this chapter. Which strategies will you try to manage your fear? Write your thoughts in the space that follows.

_____

_____

_____

_____

_____

More specifically, break down your action plan into small steps. Focus on one aspect of your sexual hesitancy. To organize your thoughts, complete the following statement:

The next time I find myself in a sexually intimate situation, I'd like to try to manage my shyness by:

_____

_____

_____

_____

_____

_____

_____

_____

WHAT'S YOUR COURAGE SCORE?

First, let's look at your courage score for being verbally shy around people you know. On a scale of 1 to 10, with 1 being the courage of a kitten (while at a museum you rent the audio tour guide instead of exploring the exhibits with your date), and 10 the courage of a lion (walking in the park on your fourth date, you feel comfortable with the conversational flow), rate your verbal intimacy courage score. Circle your score below.

1 1.5 **2** 2.5 **3** 3.5 **4** 4.5 **5** 5.5 **6** 6.5 **7** 7.5 **8** 8.5 **9** 9.5 **10**

You may wish to write your score in the space that follows: _____

If your score is more kitten than lion—perhaps it's 4.5—ask yourself what you can incorporate from your action plans to increase your score to 5. The next time you find yourself in a verbally intimate situation, try to bring your courage score up another half point by attempting—or even imagining—one of the cognitive and/or behavioral courage steps suggested in this and previous chapters. For example, instead of very quiet dinners with the television on and very little conversation, you might try watching a show that could stimulate discussion.

Now, score your sexual courage. On a scale of 1 to 10, with 1 being the courage of a kitten (you canceled your fifth date with a man you'd really started to like because you had a feeling it would have been your first night "together") and 10 the courage of a lion (you actually suggested to your lover what he can do to better please you), rate your sexual intimacy courage score. Circle your score below.

1 1.5 **2** 2.5 **3** 3.5 **4** 4.5 **5** 5.5 **6** 6.5 **7** 7.5 **8** 8.5 **9** 9.5 **10**

You may wish to write your score in the space that follows: _____

If your score is more kitten than lion—perhaps it's 5.5—ask yourself what you can incorporate from your action plans to increase it to a 6. The next time you find yourself in a sexually intimate situation, try to bring your courage score up another half point by attempting—or even imagining—one of the cognitive and/or behavioral courage steps suggested in this and previous chapters, such as humorously admitting in the bedroom, "Uh-oh. I'm having a shyness attack."

The sensual can be such a joyous part of life that not to enjoy it fully is a huge loss. We're all built to desire that sense of oneness with another person. If you're prone to saying, "It's okay. I don't need sex that much," I hope this chapter has given you strategies for pushing through the barrier of fear. It's not easy, but taking small steps, even half steps, is the definition of success. And overall, to increase your intimate and sexual confidence, I encourage you to keep practicing. To break through intimacy shyness, don't be afraid to experiment. You learn to do things by doing them.

{TEN}

NAVIGATING THE ONLINE SINGLES SCENE

ONLINE DATING HAS BECOME SUCH A POPULAR WAY to meet people that it's impossible for shy singles to ignore this as an option. According to comScore Media Metrix, a Web tracking service, at last count, 45 million people visited these sites monthly. Just think of all the single men and women out there who are a mere click of the mouse away. Indeed, Internet dating is a relief and an aid for many shy singles because the first, often precarious, stage of a relationship is safely between them and their computers. "When you start off dating online, you can really get to know someone. Your wants are less likely to block what's there because the actual person isn't in front of you," said Malcolm, a shy stockbroker in his fifties.

The online phenomenon is truly a boon to the dating scene. One of its biggest advantages is that you can go mate shopping and browse as long as you wish before committing yourself. The abundance of other date seekers on the Internet can help you feel less alone in your quest. Moreover, you can ease your way into meeting someone face to face, which is a bonus if you're shy around people you don't know. One of my workshop participants, Stella, corresponds for months before she graduates to talking on the phone, then meeting in person. By the time she had a face-to-face rendezvous with someone with whom she had been e-mailing for two months, she "knew his favorite foods, what he likes to do in his spare time, that he was raised by a single mother, and how his boss is making him crazy," she said. "But even more important than what I knew about him is our rapport because we had been chatting for so long. He wasn't a stranger and I didn't feel as self-conscious as I think I would have if I were meeting him for the first time without such a lengthy introduction. You get a better view of the person when you start off corresponding," she concluded.

> **COACH'S CORNER**
>
> Many Shys must spend time getting used to unfamiliar roles, whether it be dating online, learning to ski, or shopping at a store they've never been in before (especially one in which they imagine the sales staff to be snobby or unfriendly). That said, I often encourage my workshop participants to give Internet dating a try for three months before they decide whether it's right for them—or not. For a current list of online dating sites to which you might subscribe, simply type "dating" into a search engine and do your own research from there.

Since so many singles are signing up with online dating services, the desperate stigma once associated with Internet dating has given way to "Why not give it a try?" And why not? Internet dating offers you one more avenue to explore. Compared to traditional avenues, such as set-ups, combing the bar scene, and taking classes, it's an easy way to increase your exposure and put yourself on the dating map.

Still, online dating isn't without its difficulties. In fact, some shy singles find it stressful at every juncture—from writing the profile and responding when they're contacted, to the first phone call and actual meeting. "You wonder, 'Is this person for real? Does he sound like he's the sort of guy he says he is? What is he really interested in—sex or a relationship?'" Stephanie said to the group one evening. She had a point. Even though you may start out "dating" in the coziness of your own home, online relationships take savvy—and courage—each step of the way, from the initial hello to the first face-to-face meeting . . . and beyond.

Increasing Your Connectivity

If you're *not* new to online dating, take a moment to reflect on your e-dating experiences. Have shyness attacks been an issue for you? If so, what stages are particularly challenging—the fear of initiation when you first contact someone or meet in person? Do you experience freezing or flooding when e-mailing or in person? Do you agonize post-correspondence or after meeting up with someone one on one? Write your answers below.

The biggest hurdles I tend to face with online dating are:

WRITING THE AD

If you decide to join the ranks of the millions who sign on to the Internet, there are several key strategies to help you manage all stages of a shyness attack. If you're new to the online dating scene, you may be tempted to simply write your ad, then wait for responses to flood your e-mail inbox. I encourage you to take a more proactive approach. Like dating off-line, you can miss out on many opportunities if you simply sit back and let the parade pass you by.

Take comfort in the fact that you can first browse the ads to see if you find one or two people you're interested in before joining the dating service and sending them a message. As your courage increases, you may decide to bump up your contact quota to five or six people. "Dating online is a numbers game," said Raquel, a thirty-three-year-old media planner who dated more than 100 men in less than six months until she finally met someone who was "just right."

Going online isn't as scary as you might imagine. Here are some tips to guide you through the process.

First, mentally prepare. If you're like many Shys I know, you may need a pep talk before. This is why I suggest psyching yourself up by making a list of your positive qualities along with any new beliefs or affirmations you'd like to incorporate into your dating strategy. (You may have already started if you listed your dating goals in chapter two.) For her positive-quality list, Gail, a fiftyish divorced mother of one, wrote: thoughtful, funny, organized, loyal, sensitive, friendly, and "I'm a good catch." For her dating strategy, she wrote, "I'm looking for a man who strives for a balanced life whose words match his actions." Gail's dating "guidelines," as she called them, resulted from her failed marriage to a workaholic and several relationships that soured because she was frequently told one thing ("I think I'm falling in love with you"), but received another (countless Saturday nights alone). Read your qualities and affirmations aloud to solidify them in your mind before you start writing.

Secondly, organize your thoughts by making two lists: the things you think others should know about you, and the qualities you're looking for in a potential mate. In both columns, put down anything that comes to mind. (Save editing for later.) Take your time. Once you think you're done with your lists, put them

COACH'S CORNER

Some of my shy clients say that when writing a personal ad, they don't even hint at sex. "Why state the obvious?" said Carla, a computer programmer in her early forties. "It's implied that if you should hook up with someone online, meet in person, and hit it off, intimacy is probably in the offing somewhere down the line, as it would be if you met in low-tech ways—at a bar, through friends, or at work." She had a point, but on the other hand, you need to judge for yourself. If your inclination is to tease about sex, then go with your instinct (but be prepared for the sex-seeking responses you'll likely receive).

aside to let them "marinate" for a couple hours or even days. As you go about your life, other things may come to mind, which you can then add to your growing compilation. And for now, don't worry about the "logistics" of your ad—for example, your age, occupation, your likes and dislikes.

Go easy on the list of "must haves" for the person you seek. Unless you know for sure, for example, that you must meet a fellow nonsmoking Armenian attorney who square dances, it could be better to cast a wide net and describe the general qualities you seek.

This approach worked for Janet, a fortyish bookkeeper. She merely requested a man who is "financially stable who likes to travel and linger over gourmet meals." "Since I'm shy, I feed off talkers," she explained. "Quiet men bring out my reticence." Traveling and dialogue were high on her list, but the rest she left to chance.

Be specific in your profile. Some people feel that you should mention age, occupation, whether or not you have children, whether you're looking for a date or a life partner, and your interests, which could be automatic jumping-off points for later conversation and may send strong connecting signals to kindred spirits. This school of thought says that the more specific, the better. If you like to read, what genre? If you love music, what kind? If you're a sports fan, what teams and why? If you like to cook, what's your specialty? My shy single clients who are oriented towards specifics would also encourage avoiding clichés—

the kind that elicit a "Who doesn't?" response. In New York City, for example, it's common to say in an online ad: "Enjoy relaxing over the Sunday *New York Times* with a steamy cappuccino." (Who doesn't?) Another common ad might read, "Enjoy long walks on the beach at sunset." (Who doesn't?) The school of specifics encourages letting your true self shine through in the details and thinking long and hard about including those that really say something about you. Just two or three telling details will do; there's no need to go on and on. Better to leave a little for your readers to discover.

Remember the golden rule. In writing your ad, don't include anything to which you personally wouldn't feel comfortable responding. Kendrick, the shy actor from chapter four, wrote in his online ad: "I'd love to spend evenings by the fireplace with a special person or sitting on the edge of the dock with our feet in the water, sipping margaritas." When he reviewed his ad with the group, he realized that if he read that ad from somebody else, he wouldn't re-

COACH'S CORNER

One strategy some of my Shys use is to downplay their assets—even highlight their faults. "That way, your date can think you're not half as bad as you make yourself out to be if you should meet in person," said Valerie, a Shy in her mid-thirties. That doesn't mean mentioning your snoring, your bunions, and your fondness for cigars. Save those for later; it will all come out in due time. It also doesn't mean telling potential suitors anything that could conjure up the idea that you believe you're a "bad" person, such as anything you feel guilty about. This could give the impression that you need others to reassure you (a red flag). But you may also decide to issue warning shots about things that aren't likely to change in the near future, such as the fact that you just invested in a new home and have no plans to leave your small town. Also, be upfront about personal facts that are likely to affect potential relationships, such as the fact that you work long hours, have custody of children, are between jobs, or smoke. These are not necessarily "bad" things—in fact, they may even attract certain people to you (such as fellow smokers)—but they're characteristics that could be deal breakers for some people. Better to be out with it to avoid wasting everyone's time—yours and your potential date's.

spond to it because it would engender a major case of fear of initiation. "I don't know if I could live up to such romantic expectations," he said. Kendrick, on second thought, deleted that fantasy segment from his profile.

Mention your shyness. If you tend to be bold with the written word, clueing potential Internet dates in to your personality, even in the very first e-mail, may ease the fear of initiation and alleviate potential confusion when a meeting takes place or when/if you become more intimate at some later date. Although you don't have to mention your shyness right in your profile, you might—or just hint at it in your e-mail correspondence by writing something like, "I'm a little quiet at first, but once I get to know someone, I'm off and running," or "I'm somewhat reserved initially, but quite the opposite when I'm comfortable in my surroundings." Laurie, a pharmaceutical salesperson in her mid-thirties, chose to mention her shyness in her profile: "I think you should know that I'm shy when I first meet someone. People often comment that I'm nothing like my online persona—and I'm okay with that." If you're shy around people you know, you could even say something like, "I come on strong in the beginning, but simmer down once I get to know someone."

If you neglect to mention your shyness, when you finally meet your e-dates, your online image may not match your real one. That can be true whether you're shy or not, but perhaps more so if you're shy. (And if your date is surprised by that one disparity, he might think there are others in the pipeline.) Hank, a thirty-nine-year-old researcher for a credit ratings agency, described Martha, a woman with whom he had been corresponding for three months. "Although I felt less shy than I have on other, more traditional dates, I was still a little reserved. I wasn't my witty and charming online self, and Martha commented, 'You don't seem anything like you do online.' I could tell she was disappointed and so was I for being that way. I wish I had warned her." (After dating for two months, things were going well because the sex was very satisfying. Down the road, they will probably have to deal with Hank's reticence to speak, but after all his practice, he's better prepared for that eventuality.)

Draft your profile in a word processing program. Otherwise, if you write your ad online, you may feel rushed and might not present your best self or advertise for the kind of person you'd really like to meet. Now's the time to consider logistics, or other points worth mentioning in your essay, such as your career, your main interests outside of work, your life goals, how you like to spend free time, and any general personality traits you're looking for in a mate. To make your ad stand out, you might also mention a remarkable quality, trait, or life-altering experience you've had. That's what Fiona did. Although only twenty-seven, Fiona, an insurance administrator, had already been a foster parent to three infants. She wrote about that in her ad and noted, "I was surprised about how much I loved each baby the second they were placed in my arms." That said a lot about her. Gary, a forty-three-year-old computer consultant, chose to mention how his priorities changed after 9/11. "The old me worked eighteen hours a day and crashed on weekends. The new me works ten hours a day, hangs out with friends, ventures outside even when it's freezing, and never eats at a desk, no matter how busy I get."

Print your draft and edit it again, put it aside, add and edit, and so on. Finally, when you *love* what you've written, you might consider getting a perspective from one or two

COACH'S CORNER

When writing their online profiles, some of my workshop participants report that they avoid trying to impress readers with quirky fonts and unconventional capitalization, which can send a confusing message and make them seem scattered. "That's how I feel when I read the ads of people who do that," said Tim, a shy single in his early forties who had been online dating for a year. Instead, my clients recommend having your ad stand out with demonstrations of your personality. "Think substance over style," Tim said. Of course, your own imagination and creativity may lead you to experiment with your expression—you'll know you're on the right track when your online essay and answers feel authentic to you.

HANDLING INTERNET INTIMACY

Many of the shy singles in my workshops ultimately decide to play the numbers game and date as many of the people they meet online as they can in a given number of months. "At thirty-five, it's a strategy I'm trying because I feel like I'm reaching my expiration date," said Debra, a gerontologist who longs to have children. If you go that route, do have a policy in place concerning physical contact (even kissing). Do you wait for the special someone who truly wins your heart? Or do you peck some on the cheek, some on the lips, say goodnight with a handshake to some and a hug to others? What about further intimacy?

As I mentioned in chapter seven, if you're shy, you have to be particularly definitive about establishing your personal boundaries with yourself. Then kindly yet firmly communicate this nonnegotiable position to your online dates when meeting in person for the first time, just like you would with someone you met another way. The main problem some of my shy clients experience with online dating is how easy it is to send mixed messages. It's tempting, for example, to be flirtatious online or even respond flirtatiously to someone who's initiating the exchange and then find yourself in the uncomfortable position of being expected to keep up the banter or "deliver the goods" when you meet in person. Troy, an investment banker in his mid-forties, felt he went so far afield from his actual, understated persona that he was afraid to meet his online date in person. He ended up stalling indefinitely until she lost interest.

The moral is to be mindful of what you offer up about yourself. Before you press the send button, ask yourself: *Is that message me?* If the answer is no, rework your response until it better matches who you are, and do that for every message. Similarly, if your online date starts a conversational thread you're not comfortable with—such as "So, do you ever sleep with someone on the first date?"—simply say you're not comfortable talking about that sort of thing and use humor if you like ("Call me a prude, but do we have to go there?"), rather than feeling the need to continue that line of questioning.

friends before you send it out. You might consider asking someone you trust to give it a once-over. Then, cut and paste your ad and post it online.

Post a terrific photo of yourself. Some of the shy singles I work with are embarrassed about this part of the deal. They believe none of their photos is worthy of being posted to the masses. But because humans judge by appearance, posting an online photo is a necessary evil; it's also a strong selling point. In fact, a lot of people won't respond to an ad if there's not a photo attached. Chemistry is extremely important; if a potential date likes your photo, she's more likely to respond to your ad. With this in mind, your photo should be fairly recent. (If you're fifty-five, don't post a picture of yourself at forty; that's deception. But if you're fifty-five and look forty, say so.) Pick an image in which you look happy, relaxed, and natural. The photo could be one of you on vacation, for example. (If you choose a photo with you in sunglasses, however, keep in mind that some viewers may feel you're hiding something; many people feel more comfortable when they can see someone's eyes.)

Your creativity should determine your choice, so give yourself permission to take a chance. "I posted a photo of myself in a favorite cowboy hat," said Calvin, an attorney at a large Manhattan firm who had just been on vacation in Wyoming. While some workshop participants warned him that women might think he was a "Western, man's man type," Calvin was willing to take a chance. "We'll see what happens," he shrugged. (After his ad had been up only a few hours, he received several responses.)

Be forthcoming. After they finish the essay portion of their ad and scroll down to the multiple-choice questions, many Shys are adamant about avoiding canned answers, such as "I'll tell you later," as much as possible—to all but perhaps the most personal questions, such as income. Otherwise, "if you have a lot of 'I'll tell you laters,' it sounds like you're trying to hide something or be cute, which can be a turnoff," said Natasha, a twenty-three-year-old paralegal who just moved to New York from Indiana. The bottom line is, *you* decide who you want to respond to and how you do it. With trial and error, your approach can be continuously modified, depending on the reactions you get.

RESPONDING ETIQUETTE

When responding to the e-mails you receive, you may be tempted to simply ignore certain people. But don't. Give them the courtesy of a reply. Try something like, "Thanks for your interest, but no thank you. Good luck with your continued search." It might seem cold, but many people feel it's more compassionate than a nonresponse. (Imagine if you were the person on the other end, waiting.) If, however, the person is persistent and fails to take the hint, then by all means, it's okay to not respond.

For those you're clearly interested in, however, it's obviously important to answer thoughtfully. Still, if you're like some of the Shys in my workshops, figuring out what to say can be mind-boggling. "I either suddenly can't think of anything to say or I babble," said Kerri, a hairstylist who subscribed to three Internet dating services. To help her through stage two, she drafted her responses outside of e-mail, using her word processor, so she could gather her thoughts and

COACH'S CORNER

If your tendency is to e-mail for months before agreeing to meet face to face, I recommend *not* having an e-mail relationship with just one person at a time. The downside to that strategy is that if someone doesn't work out, you will have wasted a lot of your time. If you can do it, try to keep several balls in the air until you've met and you're sure you want to become exclusive. "I try to have three e-mail relationships going at once," said June, a shy single in her thirties who works in a research library. "But more than that and I'm swamped." Most of the singles I work with stick with one service at a time, but people do subscribe to several services at once or give each service a time limit, like three months, and then switch to another if the right person hasn't shown up.

then post them when she felt confident about their content. Another way to get started is to simply reveal a little bit more about yourself, then add an extra paragraph or two that relates to what the other person wrote and shows an interest in getting to know him. Once you begin volleying responses, corresponding usually becomes less self-conscious and takes on a life of its own.

The Lowdown on Lying

Because you're meeting in the anonymous cocoon of cyberspace, electronic dating offers a huge potential for lying. You can literally and "virtually" reinvent yourself. It's tempting. Some people, for example, lie about their age, claiming it's the only way to meet someone who matches their energy level. The problem with this strategy is that it's short-sighted. The truth usually comes out eventually, and when it does, your dates could feel suspicious and tricked. They may have doubts about what else you may have lied about.

This happened to Toni, an aspiring actress. She had been dating Jim for three months. They met online and corresponded for two months before meeting. The chemistry was "vavoom." Trouble was, Jim initially said he was twenty-eight, the same age as Toni. After five dates, however, he confessed that he was really only twenty-six. Toni didn't know what to believe. "Why would he lie about his age if he's only two years younger than me?" she wondered. She asked Jim that same question. "He said he didn't want me to *not* go out with him because I had mentioned that I was looking for someone at least my age," Toni said. It made sense, but that primary lie colored everything. Did Jim really graduate from Columbia like he said he did? Was he really *not* seeing anybody else? Was he really twenty-six? "I'm confused," said Toni, who had fallen hard for Jim. "I feel like hiring a private detective," she said, only half joking.

The fact is, lying may erode trust, the foundation of any relationship. And once you do it, there's often no easy way to right

COACH'S CORNER

If you're fooled or taken in by someone who remains less than honest, study what that means about yourself. All experiences can be enlightening. It's not the end of the world. You will get to have another chance with someone else. The beauty of dating online is its abundance of choices. As my grandmother was fond of saying, "Live and learn." And how true that is with any form of dating. You can try again. You *can* do it over.

yourself. Think about the consequences before you decide to fudge the truth because you can't take it back, which is thorny for anyone but especially so if you're shy. It's better to be honest, even if you think the truth is not what your potential dates want to hear. If it's your age you're concerned about, for example, you could just take a risk and say it, let your photo do the talking, or consider giving a general range like "late twenties" or "mid-forties." Chances are, your date won't ask exactly how old you are until after she's gotten to know you better and by then, it may not matter. (Age tends to lose its importance when it's not just a number.) But if your age does bother your date, it's better to know earlier in the relationship rather than later, when you may have become seriously attached.

Conversely, even though it's best to make a pact with yourself to honestly represent who you are, that doesn't mean others have decided to be truthful. It's human nature to want to paint yourself in the best light, but you have the right to expect 100 percent honesty. His words should match his actions.

MEETING IN PERSON

Even if you chat with someone for months online, which I don't recommend since you won't know if there's physical chemistry, you can still experience the fear of initiation when you finally meet, just like you might if you hadn't e-mailed first. After all, first anythings are tough. To ease first-time nerves, some of my workshop participants prepare three icebreaker topics to talk about that they e-mail to their dates ahead of time. Some examples: "The five items I can't live without," "My favorite foods and why," "The most memorable thing I did last summer," or, on a more serious note, "Why I think my last relationship didn't work out." If your intuition tells you to go for it, you might also try to let her in on some of the roadblocks in your life so that she gets a chance to really interact with the person with whom she has been corresponding. A statement to complete along this line might be "What I'm up against in life right now."

Otherwise, the same rules apply to first dates with people you met online as they do to other types of dates. If you feel it's up to you to ask for the date, hedge your bets against rejection by keeping the first meeting short, inexpensive, and public. Coffee at a local café for a half hour before another appointment, for example, is one low-impact way for face time (and remember to be up-front that you have a meeting and only a half hour to talk so your date doesn't feel rejected when you start gathering your things after thirty minutes).

Here are a few more tips that might fend off the fear of asking for the date: Tell yourself, "What do I have to lose? If she says no, maybe she's shyer than I am." Even so, if she says no, ask again. ("How does your schedule look next Thursday?") If you get another no, then move on, or, if you feel bold,

COACH'S CORNER

The same strategy for not meeting at all applies to ending it with someone you met online and then later, in person. If you decide you're not a love match, simply e-mail him, "It was nice to meet you, but I don't think we're going to work as a couple." The courageous and humane approach is to at least e-mail a "thanks, but no thanks" send-off. Since you began your relationship on e-mail, ending it that way has a balance to it. (Though you might not want to face doing it, remember that you are showing compassion for the other person, which is always a good skill to develop.) Being on the receiving end of good-byes that are abrupt is also inevitable, but keep in mind that the best remedy is only a date away.

address it with that person. You could say, for example, "Okay, I can take a hint. You don't want to go out with me. But how can you be certain if we've never even met in person?" (By the way, be prepared to address this kind of persistence from those who ask *you* out, when you may be uninterested.) Keep in mind there's no harm in asking for a date (and asking again), especially early on, when you're both still essentially anonymous.

Conversely, if, over time, you decide that you *don't* want to meet someone with whom you've been corresponding, then be honest. Simply write to your online suitor that you don't sense that special something telling you to take it to the next step. "If your date persists by writing something like, 'Come on, don't you at least want to meet me?' say something like, 'No, I don't want to waste your time.' Then wish him well," said Cornelia, a shy twenty-something who had been Internet dating for five months.

A Checklist for Preparing to Meet

Just because you've been corresponding with your online date doesn't mean you're immune to a shyness attack. Here's a checklist of reminders for fending off the fear of initiation and circuit overload. (More on payback later.) If you'd like, rank these from 1 to 8, with 1 being the easiest for you to do, and 8 the most challenging. Then attempt them on the various e-dates you schedule, starting with the one that's easiest for you. Your ranking will be used to enhance your courage score, which we'll discuss at the end of the chapter.

Fending off the fear of initiation:

1. Role-play. Imagine walking up to your date and saying something friendly like, "Hi, I'm Jane. Nice to finally meet you in person." You'll be more likely to repeat the performance when the time comes. First impressions count, even if you're already well-acquainted online.

    RANK _____

2. Wear a conversation starter and see if that sparks conversation. Take note that even accessories say something about you. Messages are sent in all forms.

RANK _____

3. Be conversationally prepared. You might equip yourself with three icebreaking topics *and* brush up on your current events, recent movies you've seen, or books you've read. Also, consider asking questions that pertain to your e-mail conversations.

RANK _____

4. Reveal more about yourself through an anecdote or something that happened to you recently, if it relates to the subject at hand. It may invite your listener to do the same. In fact, have an anecdote in mind and rehearse so you'll feel confident when the time comes.

RANK _____

Short-circuiting overload:

5. Name the stage while it's happening: *Oh, there I go again, into circuit overload.* As you may recall, it's an effective way to detach from the stage while it's happening in order to derail the fear that's propelling it

RANK _____

6. Repeat a self-affirming mantra, such as *I'm an interesting person. I'm an interesting person* to bolster your confidence and squelch any negative self-talk you may be hearing.

RANK _____

7. If you freeze during a conversation, remind yourself that your date probably won't even notice. Most people, espe-

(continued on page 196)

SAFETY FIRST

One major, though not always obvious, drawback to online dating is it can be risky—more so than meeting someone through friends, for example. After all, even though you get to know something about the people with whom you've been corresponding, you don't *really* know them fully. It's extremely important to protect yourself, no matter how awkward it might feel at the time. Use your best judgment, and follow these basic guidelines:

- Don't reveal any information that personally identifies you in your online profile, such as your full name or where you live, if it's anywhere other than a big city. Stick with this principle in your private e-mails for as long as it takes until you feel comfortable.

- Don't allow singles to e-mail you at your private or work e-mail address until you feel you really know them and feel comfortable. Until then, make sure your signature doesn't include your phone number or address. Meanwhile, stick with the covert communication tools provided by your dating service, which may include e-mail, a chat room, and instant messaging. Or, consider opening a dating-designated, anonymous e-mail account at any one of the Internet's free sites.

- If you feel pressured to reveal something about yourself that you'd rather keep private, think seriously about this person and whether you want to continue e-mailing. People who don't respect your boundaries are a red flag. A general rule: If you squirm, scram.

- When you meet in person, be sure to rendezvous in a public place, such as at a coffee bar, a park, or a museum, just as you would for any other type of date. Save restaurants for the second or third meeting, after you've broken the "we're finally meeting" ice. If you don't hit it off, spending an entire dinner with someone can feel like a major commitment. You may also feel safer not meeting near your home or office, although some of my shy single clients say that's too much caution. Decide for yourself, based on your comfort level.

• As you've been doing throughout your correspondence, stay alert to the signals about your date's character, intentions, and relationship potential. Little things—like whether your date is on time, what he's wearing, or what and how he orders at a bar or restaurant—can speak volumes. He could, for example, be fastidiously punctual (or habitually late) or very fashion conscious (or a grooming nightmare); he could drink excessively (or be condemning of alcohol) or be gluttonous about food (or neurotic about it); he might be overly obsessive, or maybe just unaware. Of course, the significance of these nonverbal messages depends on what they mean to you.

Sherry, a twenty-nine-year-old magazine editor, was surprised when her online date didn't want to order an appetizer with the drinks they were having in person for the first time. "It was 7:30. We were having martinis at a famous oyster house and he even said he was hungry." Then her date revealed that he never eats dinner before 8:00 P.M. and only ate salad for lunch. "He actually patted his flat stomach and said, 'trying to watch my weight,'" Sherry said. "The words 'quirky' and 'rigid' came to mind." Did she date him again? Yes, for three months. "He was cute and funny," Sherry conceded. But as time went on, it became apparent that he was very concerned about his appearance and wouldn't budge on his time-honored eating habits. Sherry, a self-described foodie, couldn't live with that. "I don't see us as a long-term thing," she managed to say on their last date.

• If you'd like to check your date out, try "googling" her at www.google.com or www.altavista.com by simply typing in her name in parentheses. But use common sense when you find a name that matches—if the name is a common one, it could be a hit or a complete miss. If you feel you need a more targeted background check, you can also purchase reports from several online companies.

cially on first dates, are focused intently on themselves and keeping up their end of the conversation.

RANK _____

8. Practice active listening. To instantly bring yourself into a conversation (or slow down to take a breath), repeat words or phrases your date says, in the form of a question. If your date says, "I had a tough day at work," you might reply, "Tough day—that's too bad. What happened?" or "Care to talk about it?" If she mentioned that she recently visited her parents in Oklahoma, you could ask, "How was your trip?" and "What was it like growing up there?"

RANK _____

Pummeling Online Payback

You're not immune to any stage of a shyness attack, even when e-mailing, so don't be surprised if payback still occurs, especially if you've been corresponding with someone for weeks or even months. As time goes on, you're apt to reveal more and more. The participants in my workshops report worrying about talking too much about past relationships, offending their online suitor by not paying more attention to something he said, or going into too much detail about the minutiae of their lives— their unemployment, their divorce, their mother's illness. If you find yourself second-guessing much of what you're writing, it may be time to meet in person so that your suitor can get a more complete picture of who you are. E-mail, after all, only reveals so much. "At some point, you've got to put a face with the writer or the voice," said Phyllis, a retired English teacher who was looking for love again at sixty.

That said, if you meet someone in person and experience payback afterwards, remember to go easy on yourself. Empathy for yourself is the road to self-acceptance. For example, if you're reflecting on a conversational moment when you couldn't think of anything to say, remind yourself that it was *not* important. Even apparantly Nonshys have known those moments. We've all been there. Your inner dialogue may be saying: *I felt so uncomfortable. I wish I'd been able to talk. I wonder why I clammed up? After all, I felt like I knew him since we'd been e-mailing for months.* So, come up with a compassionate and empathetic theory, not unlike something you'd tell a child you were trying to soothe, which could range from *Well, maybe he's shy, too* to *I was just out of words, I guess.*

Then realistically assess your date and decide whether you want to see him again. Was there a match or a mismatch? Some of my clients prefer to label their dates in three categories: "definitely a match," "maybe a match," and "definitely not a match." To further clarify your thoughts, after you categorize your date, ask yourself why (as in "why he is definitely not a match or a maybe or a definite match"), then list your reasons. This additional analysis is a healthy form of self-reflection and may cause you to switch your date to a different category.

The reason payback can be especially strong after a first meeting is because after a period of time getting to know each other by e-mail, both of your hopes are up that this could be a great match. You finally meet, and now you feel (and assume he feels) let down. As I mentioned in chapter eight, Shys tend to attribute success to luck and believe failure to be their fault. These feelings are especially strong when an e-mail relationship nosedives. Payback swiftly follows with a vengeance unless the shy person is particularly vigilant to label it and understand what is happening following a date that didn't work out

Remember, there's a strong distinction between payback and constructive assessment of the part you play in an interchange— whether it's unsuccessful or successful. Life learning is trial and error, but to gain new knowledge from an experience you must be able to critique yourself, which is a very different exercise from tearing yourself down (the former promotes learning; the latter promotes stagnation).

YOUR ACTION PLAN

Using the strategies from this chapter and throughout the book, how will you manage your online shyness attacks so they become less troublesome? A targeted plan helps you gain courage, one small step at a time. Feel free to list your ideas here.

I'd like to manage my Internet-dating shyness by:

Here are a few examples, culled from some of my clients who have tried to manage their Internet-dating shyness. First, write a boilerplate essay about yourself, then tailor it and send it to one person a day for a month. Meanwhile, make it your mission to call three people you really like within the second week of e-mailing, and so on. "Go for volume, at first. Then prune as you go along," suggested Cameron, a pharmaceutical sales rep in his late forties. Since Internet dating can be confusing, you might want to devise a tracking system if you find yourself juggling more than three e-dates at a time. "I keep a log on my computer, with notes to myself about specific people I meet online," Cameron said.

WHAT'S YOUR COURAGE SCORE?

We complete this chapter with your courage score. On a scale of 1 to 10, with 1 being the courage of a kitten (you completed your online profile, but just couldn't bring yourself to broadcast it) and 10 the courage of a lion (you recently made a date with someone you've been corresponding with for months), rate your online dating courage score. Circle your score below.

1 1.5 **2** 2.5 **3** 3.5 **4** 4.5 **5** 5.5 **6** 6.5 **7** 7.5 **8** 8.5 **9** 9.5 **10**

You may wish to write your score in the space that follows: _____

If your score is more kitten than lion, ask yourself what you can incorporate from your action plans to increase your score just one half point. The next time you find yourself online, try to bring your courage score up another half point by attempting— or even imagining—one of the cognitive and/or behavioral courage steps I suggested in this and previous chapters, such as signing up with an online service, then crafting your profile off-line. If you're wavering at all, it's a good starting point that can help you decide whether this venue is truly right for you.

And keep in mind that every relationship that starts online increases your courage score. Give yourself credit for every connection you make. Even those that don't pan out give you a chance to practice your shyness management strategies, hone your dating skills, and increase your confidence. Whenever you revisit Internet dating, recalculate your courage score. As you take on more and more of these exercises, your score will improve.

"Being deeply loved by someone gives you strength, while loving someone deeply gives you courage."

—Lao Tzu

{ELEVEN}

BUILDING A FUTURE

As YOU PRACTICE THE SHYNESS-ATTACK management exercises throughout this book, you may soon achieve a measure of success: dates and more opportunities to meet others. But that doesn't mean your challenges are over, as Nancy, a workshop participant who works in magazine publishing, discovered. "Now, I find myself wrestling with big-picture questions, such as: 'Will I do better in the long run with guys who are shy like me, or are more outgoing, aggressive men more 'my type'?" Nancy still hadn't dated enough to know for sure. But she raises a good point. What are the pluses and minuses of pairing up with someone who is seemingly your opposite? Will such a match have staying power—or eventually become too draining and fizzle out? Would it actually be better in the long run to partner with someone who is also on the quiet side, just like you? Or will you eventually feel frustrated because no one is "the leader"?

It's tough to predict such outcomes because it's not just you and the personalities of the people you date that factor into the equation. Your upbringing and your parental role models also in-fluence your choice in a mate. If, for example, you had a father who was assertive and outspoken, you may unconsciously look for those qualities in the men you meet because they're "fa-miliar." By the same token, if your mother is on the quiet side, such women may inherently be more appealing to you on some level. Of course, birth order and other mitigating factors may also influence your decision.

But the best way to discover who works for you is to put yourself out there. By dating, you can acquire information about yourself that can then help you make conscious, benefi-cial choices. Findings could include: "I do better with men who aren't shy, who can help draw me out of myself" or "I need a woman who isn't too aggressive, otherwise I feel overpowered." Dating provides invaluable "on-the-job" experience you can't get any other way, which is why I encourage my clients to go for quantity—to date at every reasonable opportunity. In doing so, you'll be able to road-test your ideas about who is and isn't right for you. As you grow more certain with every subsequent date and you finally settle on one person in particular, you'll be more confident in your feelings for that person. The parade of candidates who precede the person you choose will help you know yourself better. An added bonus is that, later on, you'll be less likely to look back, wishing you had done more "research."

Moreover, it pays to begin a serious commitment with your eyes wide open to the problems that may occur. (Unavoidable problems, of course, such as illness, occur in every couple's life if they stay together long enough. The upside is that rough patches provide opportunities for gaining wisdom.) Still, what's down the road for you if you choose someone who is more like you or someone who seems your opposite? Let's take a peek into the future. As with most things in life, "forewarned is fore-armed."

WHEN YOUR PARTNER ISN'T SHY

Pros:

1. Whenever there's a social event, you can rely on your more extroverted partner to serve as your buddy; he can introduce you and make conversation when you feel shy.

2. She'll welcome the limelight; as a result, you'll feel less pressured.

3. He'll fill in any conversational lulls. "Whenever my husband gets quiet, that's when I worry," chuckled Selma, a former shy client of mine who is married to a "talker."

4. She'll feel comfortable initiating sex (unless she happens to be shy in bed).

5. He'll probably be the one to arrange the social dates with other couples, which takes the demand to initiate off of you.

6. She can do all of the extemporaneous speaking if you're at a dinner or an event where one of you is expected to say something.

7. He can deal with any delivery or service person, such as a housekeeper, which is an added bonus if there's a conflict.

8. She can take care of skirmishes between your parents or hers if tension arises.

9. He can make sure you always have fun. "Joey handles the social schedule, and it's always filled," said Christine, a formerly shy single who is married to a high school gym teacher/summer camp counselor.

10. She's comfortable with spontaneity and less worried about making mistakes. As a result, her "go with the flow" or "enjoy the moment" attitude may wash off on you, and you may become generally less worried.

In all, your extroverted partner can serve as an excellent teacher. He's the yin to your yang. She can exemplify the advantages of being less controlled by shyness and more in touch with the courageous side of yourself. With this type of partner, his strengths are your weaknesses, and vice versa. "We feel balanced," said Chloe, a thirty-nine-year-old music teacher who is in such an "opposites" marriage.

What You Offer Such a Person

You're a constant source of quiet security. No matter what kind of adventures your partner has, you're always there, ready to support his explorations and accept his mistakes. And even if you're not so forgiving on the inside, you often let things pass because you're hesitant to verbalize every glitch. You tend to choose your arguments carefully. Rarely could you be considered a nagging partner. A long-term plus for you in such a relationship is that over time, you become more and more appreciated by your partner, children, and others who benefit from your quiet, steady comfort.

Cons:

1. During a social event, you may be overshadowed by her exuberance. And long-term, being the moon to someone else's sun can become wearing, even depressing. Over time, as some of her courage rubs off on you, you may feel resentful of your invisibility and long to "bust out."

2. You may be considered unfriendly or dry compared to his juiciness. "People like John, but they just tolerate me," said Ana, a quiet person who married "a live wire."

3. You may begin to feel invisible in her presence in situations where you don't want to be invisible, like when visiting your parents, at your business events, or when you're with *your* crowd. "At a friend's house recently, my wife, Susan, did all the talking while I just sat there, drinking my beer.

That was fine, but they're considered my friends, not hers. Afterwards, one of my buddies came up to me and said, 'Hey, is something wrong? You're so quiet.' That bothered me," said Ken, the shy one of the couple. "That was a wake-up call. At first, I didn't know what he was talking about. I guess I'm just so used to Susan holding court."

4. He may have a tendency to ask for sex when you aren't ready or in the mood. You may get few opportunities to initiate.

5. You're usually going out with her friends and get to see yours less often.

6. You rarely receive the opportunity to develop your public speaking skills.

7. You don't practice honing your conflict resolution skills with shopkeepers and household help.

8. You're diverted from working out tensions between you and your parents or your in-laws. That can leave you feeling like a child. "My father-in-law actually said to me, 'Why don't you speak for yourself?'" said Marianne, a shy nurse married to a doctor. "I was so embarrassed."

9. You don't often get to be the social director and feel the sense of accomplishment associated with "running the show."

10. Your partner may develop the tendency to speak for you. "When a friend called the other day, wondering if I was interested in going to the gym, my husband, who answered the phone, said 'it was the weekend, and not a good day for that,'" said Karen, a shy person married to an outspoken salesman. "I was out, running an errand at the time. My friend and I laughed about it later, because it sounded like 'No, Karen can't come out and play.' We went to the gym anyway."

Making It Work

Long-term, if you begin to feel more courageous, thanks, in part, to your outgoing partner, you'll want to exert your power and practice your new skills. To keep your significant other from taking over, communication is key. A gentle, "Honey, I'll handle that one," may be all you need to say (although perhaps repeatedly). If that doesn't get the message across, you may wish to have "boundary" talks about what he can be in charge of and what you'll want to "run" in your relationship. Chances are, on one hand he'll be glad to be relieved of so much of the family responsibility, especially after he experiences how much more relaxing it can be to let someone else take charge (for a change). On the other hand, he may miss the control-power aspects of being the responsible one.

A warning: In your initial attempts to change the established patterns between you, a period of conflict could ensue. There's an expression that says that to have a real understanding, two people must first go through a period of misunderstanding. With that in mind, shying away from immediate moments of unpleasantness can lead to larger problems if the topic you're avoiding is extremely important to you—such as not wanting to be drowned out by another person when you're prepared to emerge. For most couples, ultimately this tension, handled lovingly and with compassion, will give way to a more exciting and dynamic relationship.

WHEN YOUR PARTNER IS ALSO SHY

Pros:

1. You both understand the shy experience without having to explain it—again and again and again. "I feel validated because Amy's a kindred spirit," said Cameron, a shy newlywed married to someone who is shy as well.

2. You both naturally love peacefulness and may enjoy doing "quiet" things like reading, doing crossword puzzles, or browsing at bookstores. On the other hand, you may also like "boisterous" activities like rock concerts and roller coasters. Either way, since your temperaments are similar, it may be easy to find activities you both enjoy.

3. Because your partner is shy, you have to push *yourself* to interact with others for the benefit of both of you, thereby expanding your social skills.

4. You never feel drowned out or invisible in your partner's company.

5. You have few yelling and screaming conflicts. "In our household, things are generally mellow," said Camille, a shy administrative assistant married to an architect she described as "an observer."

6. You often have the same point of view about rearing children, which creates a consistent parental front. "My ex-husband was a yeller, and I was constantly reminding him that he was teaching the kids to yell by his example," said Natalie, a former workshop participant. "But my second husband is on the shy side, like I am, and he's much more low-key with the kids, which is good because they yell a lot less, too. The noise level in our house has dropped three decibels."

7. Neither of you is likely to stray; loyalty is a high priority for many Shys. Once you become his love object, you're there for life.

8. As a result of the loyalty factor—and the fact that you know how tough it can be to find someone with whom to share your life—you may be more likely to work through a relationship crisis such as unfaithfulness. Even if there's a period of acting out dissatisfaction by slipping out of the marriage, you're likely to use this event to find out what's really amiss and heal the rift.

9. As a couple, your mutual desire to stick together will make you well-equipped to deal with other bumps in the road as well, such as lack of money, illness, unemployment, or the death of a parent. Neither of you is apt to bolt because your togetherness—and your mutual shyness—is a powerful glue.

10. To keep the lines of communication flowing, you may find yourself becoming more verbal. "Since both of us kind of live in our heads, sometimes either my wife or I use our code phrase 'out with it,'" said Charles, a shy academic married to a fellow shy academic (they met in college). "That means, 'Let's stop reading and talk,'" he said. "Or, 'I can tell something's bothering you. What is it?'"

What You Offer Such a Person

Your similar personality offers validation, safety, stability, and a like-mindedness that can serve you both especially well when times get tough. Through thick and thin, you're a team player.

Cons:

1. No one initiates sex. While you're waiting for the other to make a move, even if you're comfortable in other parts of your relationship, it's possible that due to the fear of initiation, nothing happens in the bedroom for months and months. (Although, once the sex gets started, it may be wonderful.) Still, your sex life may be prone to drought cycles. During these periods, you may find yourself wondering if something is wrong with your relationship.

2. No one makes dates with others. You can find yourselves lonely, even though you're married. "I wish Stan would take more interest in our social schedule," said Charlotte, a Shy who is married to a man who wishes she'd do the same.

3. When there's a conflict, the silent treatment can go on for days, and the dispute may never get resolved.

4. You get to try fewer new experiences because neither of you love experimenting or change.

5. There's no built-in buddy system if you're at a large gathering. Although your mate is alongside you, all you may do is find yourselves talking to each other. Moreover, as a couple, you could be overlooked, for example, not getting invited to neighborhood gatherings.

6. Your double shyness could affect your careers and your livelihoods if neither of you have an assertive personality. As a result, both of you may be reluctant to do what's necessary to advance, such as ask for a raise or promotion or move to a new job when necessary.

7. If you have an aggressive child, neither of you may be able to exercise a strong hand in dealing with her; she may become tyrannical around adults and bullying toward other children.

8. There are few peaks and valleys; your life together may be so smooth and quiet, it could become boring. Nobody wants a lulling gentle rain to fall all the time.

9. Your partner doesn't force you to speak, express yourself, grow verbally and emotionally. If you're not being pushed, it could feel as if you're stagnating or being ignored. "When I get quiet, Robert asks me why," said Rena, whose previous boyfriend never confronted her when she withdrew. "On that basis alone, Robert seems to be a much better match for me because we resolve things much sooner. I appreciate his candidness."

10. Since both of you are loyal, it's hard to leave even if you want to end the relationship. You can feel "stuck" and spend many years feeling like you should move on, but somehow can't.

Making It Work

Long-term, to keep your shyness from hemming you in as a couple, you'll both need to take responsibility for widening your social circle, taking more initiative in all aspects of your lives, and injecting excitement where necessary. For inspiration, some shy couples select friends who are "doers" or "movers and shakers" and take their cues from them. They selectively adopt tactics the same way you learn (as an individual) to manage dating-related shyness—that is, one small step at a time. "We make an effort to invite at least one other couple out to dinner every month, which is a stretch for us," said Ad, a married father of one. "But we've found that it has really enriched our relationship." To casually increase your exposure to others, you might also join a group, such as a local church, synagogue, or mosque, or take a class together as a couple, such as bridge or tango lessons.

HOW DO YOU KNOW WHEN YOU'VE MET "THE ONE"?

That's an important question my shy clients, especially those who have become more lion than kitten, pose to me all the time. They think they might have met someone they can spend their life with. They've been using the strategies I outline in this book and in my workshops, dating one special person for a while, and things seem to be going well. But they're not sure. "Other couples who eventually got divorced probably felt like they met 'the one,' right?" they ask. It's a niggling thought. Most of us don't want to find ourselves having to start over. If you're shy, this is an especially difficult change to tolerate. When thinking about the future, it may feel like it could take forever to get used to a new situation and feel comfortable committing again.

Of the countless shy singles in my workshops who have found significant others, their courtships and engagements have tended to proceed slowly. "We dated for nearly four years before we finally got married," said Denise, a Shy who was deathly afraid to walk down the aisle. Her fear was that all eyes would be on her, yet she didn't want to be deprived of a storybook wedding—white gown, bridesmaids, the whole thing. "But one day, when the desire to marry Thomas became stronger than my fear of the limelight, I realized that it just felt right to me to marry, so we set a wedding date." For Denise, time helped her feel confident about their relationship. "I used my issue as a test. I wanted to make sure it felt solid between us before I committed," she said.

In general, you will know when you have met "the one" either one of two ways:

It will be nearly instant recognition, a feeling of comfort, a feeling of "where have you been my whole life?" A feeling you've found your soul mate, that you must have met in another lifetime. Or . . .

You'll slowly "grow on" each other, like Denise and Thomas. Your chemistry may be a slow burn that develops right along with trust. In time, you'll begin to feel as if you fit with this other person, that your day-to-day interactions seem to increasingly flow with the ease of a winding stream. This can happen if you work together or see each other over time. Bells don't ring; your heart doesn't skip a beat; but there's an essence of familiarity, which could be instantaneous or may grow with trust, a sense that the person feels right. I knew a shy couple who were raised next door to each other; later in life, they re-met and married. "Throughout my life, I gravitated toward high-strung intellectuals like myself," said Jay, the husband. "But after I re-met Rita, who is down to earth, I came to realize that she was the woman I needed."

Good Luck on Your Journey

Meeting and choosing a life partner is a complex task, and it has never been more challenging, thanks to the fast, depersonalized pace of modern life, the myriad choices we have for lifestyles, careers, and locales, and the pressure to be proactive in all aspects of our lives. Still, you're in the driver's seat if you're out there meeting others—and practicing your shyness management skills—rather than waiting for others to come to you. You're on the right track just by choosing and reading this book.

To comprehensively organize your courage campaign, take a moment now to list the strategies I outlined for managing all three stages of a shyness attack that you found to be the most helpful. Which ones really did the trick for you? Was it actively listening? Wearing a conversation piece? Bringing a buddy to events? Thinking of yourself as someone who's there to help others? Brushing up on current events and other ice-breaking topics? List them here. What worked for you?

Consider this list your shyness attack "cheat sheet." You may want to photocopy it and keep it with you for handy reference, when you're in the heat of a shyness attack battle.

YOUR COURAGE SCORE: THE FINALE

We complete this chapter with your final courage score. Again, on a scale of 1 to 10, with 1 being the courage of a kitten and 10 the courage of a lion, rate your overall courage score. How courageous do you feel today compared to how you felt at the beginning of your courage campaign? Circle your score below, and continue to challenge yourself in the coming weeks and months to raise your courage score even just half a point at a time, toward freedom and away from the tyranny of fear.

1 1.5 2 2.5 3 3.5 4 4.5 5 5.5 6 6.5 7 7.5 8 8.5 9 9.5 10

You may wish to write your score in the space that follows: _____

Be B.R.A.V.E.

I hope you'll make it your mission to continue loosening the grip that shyness has over you. As you continue to employ the strategies throughout this book, I want to leave you with a simple mnemonic device to review from time to time or use when you need fast relief from a shyness attack. It's easy to re-member because it spells the word "brave."

Breathe. During a shyness attack, many shy people have a tendency to hold their breath, which can exacerbate anxiety symptoms. Focusing on deep breathing does two things: It sends oxygen to the brain to help alleviate symptoms, and it gives you something to do to take your mind off your emotional discomfort.

Rally. Be your own best friend. In the midst of a shyness at-tack, remember to tell yourself (*You can do this* or *I'm okay, I've done this before*), rather than give in to the fear and feelings of unworthiness, panic, and self-loathing.

Awareness. When you're experiencing a stage of a shyness at-tack, stay in the moment and call yourself on it (*Oh, there it is* *again, stage two*). By silently acknowledging it, you'll distance and detach yourself from the fear, which can give you an added edge.

Victory. Remember that you're not here to rearrange your entire emotional makeup, but to take small steps toward your goal. Each time you go out, push yourself a little bit more. Over time, you'll be rewarded for your willingness to take small risks with an energizing feeling of momentum.

Experience. This is your greatest teacher. If you try a strategy in this book, whether you're Internet dating or enjoying a wedding solo, and it doesn't work, try another and another until something clicks. (It will.) Congratulate yourself for putting yourself out there and getting that much closer to your goal—because you never know what can happen. That night, event, or e-mail message could be the start of the end of your dating career.

Good luck may be just around the corner, and to reach that corner you have to do just one thing: keep moving, one step at a time. When it comes to fostering courage, there's no substitute for experience. And on your journey, keep in mind these words from John Wayne: "Courage is being scared to death and saddling up anyway."

{APPENDIX}

WHEN IT'S MORE THAN SHYNESS

Some of my clients ask if there's a prescription medication they can take for their "condition," especially now that television advertising prominently features so many reports of people feeling dramatically better. I assure them that medication is available for social anxiety disorder—as well as other anxiety disorders, such as obsessive-compulsive disorder and panic disorder—but not for painful shyness, per se. When my clients complain that their fears are crippling them, however, I usually refer them to a psychiatrist or psychopharmacologist, because if they could benefit from medication it would only increase our chances for success.

Of these conditions, painful shyness is most frequently confused with social anxiety disorder, and for good reason. The two are first cousins. Social anxiety disorder is a disruptive condition in which sufferers are overly concerned with public scrutiny. According to the National Institute of Mental Health (NIMH), approximately 5.3 million Americans have social anxiety disorder in any given year. Sufferers of this disorder experience extreme worry about embarrassing themselves in front of others. Simply being around others can make them uncomfortable. If their fears become so impairing that they can't talk on the phone, sign a check in front of a salesclerk, use a public restroom, or they find dating or going to parties difficult and mostly avoid these situations, they have developed social phobia. Social anxiety disorder frequently runs in families and occurs more often in women than men. It also tends to begin in childhood or early adolescence and commonly afflicts primarily fearful or shy individuals—although a person can be shy without being clinically socially anxious.

Shyness, on the other hand, is considered a normal and prevalent personality trait, a tendency towards fearfulness that's influenced by genetics. Like height, it occurs naturally, with the same statistical array: some people are very short, most are in the middle, and some are very tall; this distribution is also true for shyness.

Studies show that the shy and those with social anxiety disorder can experience similar physical responses in social situations, but the degree of discomfort determines the diagnosis. Both conditions—shyness and social anxiety disorder—are governed by the amygdala, the fear center of the brain. In response to perceived stressors, such as public scrutiny, both Shys and the socially anxious may blush; their muscles may twitch; their heart may pound in their chests. Both may worry about being criticized or ridiculed. Painful shyness and social anxiety disorder can be quite severe, leading to self-deprecating thoughts, increased general anxiety, even depression. But social anxiety disorder, by definition, will compromise a person's ability to function normally in society, such that he or she avoids social situations. Shyness, on the other hand, is uncomfortable, but not usually without the hope that some days will be better than others. Although some shy singles may prefer to stay home rather than attend social events, they are able to freely make this choice. Those with social anxiety disorder may lose that ability to choose.

Another major difference between the two conditions is that the shy can learn to manage their condition without medication. With the right strategies and tactics (such as those described in this book), Shys can push through and diminish the fear factor in any given situation and slowly adjust their cautious tendencies, hone their small-talk skills, and teach themselves to modify their perceptions of themselves in comparison to others. If, on the other hand, a person truly suffers from social anxiety disorder, the intensity of the fear she experiences may interfere with acquiring these coping skills. Often medication and a specific short-term form of professional help called cognitive-behavior ("talk") therapy is also needed to make her less anxious and afraid so she can do everyday things like date, use a public restroom, or speak in public. Social anxiety disorder may be treated with cognitive-behavior therapy with no pharmaceutical assistance, but because treatment involves changing brain chemistry, progress may be slower, and the quality of a person's social life can be severely compromised while she waits for therapy to kick in.

SOCIAL ANXIETY DISORDER OR DEPRESSION?

If you believe that you suffer from social anxiety disorder, seek treatment as soon as possible and stick with it. Untreated, it can lead to restricted function, extremely compromised feelings of self-worth, and even clinical depression. Clinical depression is a serious illness that may or may not go away on its own, no matter how long you try to wait it out or "pull yourself together." In any given year, according to the NIMH, nearly 19 million Americans suffer from a depressive illness. Clinical depression may worsen over time if left untreated. Individual or group psychotherapy and/or antidepressant medication can help up to 80 percent of those with depression, usually within weeks of beginning treatment. Continued treatment helps to prevent depression from recurring.

ARE YOU A CANDIDATE FOR MEDICATION?

This question is one worth pondering because everything you ingest—from salami to psychotropic medication—could be benign, have positive consequences, or, at the extreme, produce unforeseen results. In any event, if you have social anxiety disorder, a trial of medication may be helpful in gaining the freedom and courage you're seeking. If you're suffering, medication can increase your receptivity to practicing various coping skills and exercises. To be a candidate for medication, you must receive a diagnosis and a prescription from a doctor, psychiatrist, or psychopharmacologist. Whether you have social anxiety disorder or are merely shy, ultimately you must still push past your comfort level to benefit from greatly expanded social life experiences. If you're unsure whether you're shy or actually suffering from social anxiety disorder—and therefore would benefit from medication—take the quiz on pages 220–221 to help you determine whether you need to see your doctor.

Minding Your Meds

Medication for social anxiety can help you feel more comfortable in situations that ordinarily cause anxiety. It can give you the ability to practice your new cognitive skills with less internal stress, although it doesn't permanently take away symptoms; only behavioral intervention can hope to do that. If you stop the medication without learning new skills, social anxiety will usually resume. Here is just a sampling of the many types of medication available for various forms of treatment.

- Beta-blockers, medications that stop symptoms associated with a rapid heartbeat

- Selective serotonin reuptake inhibitors (SSRIs). Some popular names for SSRIs are fluoxetine (Prozac), sertraline (Zoloft), paroxetine (Paxil), fluvoxamine (Luvox), and citalopram (Celexa)

- Monoamine oxidase inhibitors (MAOIs), such as phenelzine (Nardil) and tranylcypromine (Parnate)

- Benzodiazepines, such as lorazepam (Ativan) or the longer-lasting alprazolam (Xanax) and clonazepam (Klonopin)

- Other medications that may be prescribed for social anxiety include anti-convulsant drugs such as gabapentin (Neurontin) and antipsychotic drugs such as olanzapine (Zyprexa) and risperidone (Risperdal)

For more information about specific drugs, speak to your doctor or log on to the Web site for the National Institute of Mental Health (www.nimh.nih.gov). Click on Publication Order Form, then on Medications.

If you suspect that you're more than shy and might benefit from prescription medication, don't let another day go by without getting the help you need. Nearly two-thirds of those with a diagnosable mental disorder don't seek treatment because of the stigma associated with seeing a mental health professional for talk therapy and a psychiatrist for medication. Don't be one of them. Life is too short and precious to miss opportunities for treatment that may help you improve and recover. If you have social anxiety disorder or another mental health condition, medication, after all, is only part of your treatment plan. What you do (or don't do) still plays a significant part in helping you achieve the social life you desire.

GETTING HELP

If you have a high "yes" score on the medication quiz on pages 220–221, and social anxiety or other emotional stressors interfere with your life, there are several places you can explore to get help. If your company offers an employee assistance program (EAP), you may want to go there first. Often, the EAP has a network of mental health specialists to whom you can be re-

(continued on page 222)

TO TAKE MEDICATION OR NOT? A QUIZ TO HELP YOU DECIDE

If you're unsure whether you're merely shy or are, in fact, suffering from social anxiety disorder, obsessive compulsive disorder, or depression—and therefore a candidate for medication—your real-life experience can give you the information you need to build your case either way. But if you'd like help in deciding, take this general quiz, which I've developed based on the traits my socially anxious clients display. I use this tool to help them gauge their level of social anxiety, and with it, determine whether they need to seek medical help. To complete it, simply answer yes or no to the questions below by circling your response.

YES   NO   1. I obsess over wasting time.

YES   NO   2. I have certain rituals—like always taking an umbrella when I go outside, whether or not rain is predicted for that day.

YES   NO   3. If I wake up at night, I feel anxious and concerned that I can't sleep.

YES   NO   4. I resent my boss and family members for taking my excessive work output for granted, or not doing enough of their share.

YES   NO   5. I get angry easily and frequently find myself in conflicts with difficult people at work and/or at home.

YES   NO   6. Leaving home is so uncomfortable that I usually prefer not to face it; I remain at home as much as possible.

YES   NO   7. I prefer my bed to any other place in the world.

YES   NO   8. I drink to get through a social evening.

YES   NO   9. I find little to feel passionate about. .

YES   NO   10. I prefer the computer, television, videos, electronic games, books, and/or my pet to meeting people.

YES **NO**	11.	I'm intimidated by people in authority.
YES **NO**	12.	I blush when I'm in front of others, and it bothers me.
YES **NO**	13.	Parties and social events make me uncomfortable.
YES **NO**	14.	Being criticized scares me a lot.
YES **NO**	15.	I avoid doing things or speaking to people out of the fear of embarrassment.
YES **NO**	16.	Sweating in front of people upsets me.
YES **NO**	17.	I avoid going to parties.
YES **NO**	18.	I avoid activities in which I'm the center of attention.
YES **NO**	19.	Talking to strangers scares me.
YES **NO**	20.	I avoid having to give speeches.
YES **NO**	21.	I would do anything to avoid being criticized.
YES **NO**	22.	I have heart palpitations when I'm around others.
YES **NO**	23.	I'm afraid of doing things when people might be watching.
YES **NO**	24.	Being embarrassed or looking foolish are among my worst fears.
YES **NO**	25.	I avoid speaking to anyone in authority.
YES **NO**	26.	I tremble or shake in the presence of others.

If you answered yes to more than eight of these questions, you should seek a consultation with a psychiatrist or psychopharmacologist. If he or she concludes that you would benefit from medication, you might also request to see a therapist who is competent in treating anxiety disorders with cognitive-behavior ("talk") therapy.

ferred. It also makes sense to pay a visit to your primary care physician to make sure you have no underlying physical condition, such as diabetes, asthma, or even multiple sclerosis, that could be a stimulus for feeling anxious, fearful, or depressed.

If the problem isn't medical, your primary care physician may be able to refer you to a mental health practitioner or center. In any event, you'll want to be evaluated and diagnosed by a mental health specialist. Ideally, to achieve the greatest benefits from the miracles of modern medicine, you would be best served by working with a psychopharmacologist, a medical doctor who specializes in psychiatry and whose training includes the study of medication that aids in achieving emotional balance. You can log on to the Web site for the American Psychiatric Association (www.psych.org) for the names of psychopharmacologists and qualified psychiatrists in your area. Other resources to turn to include the department of psychiatry at a local hospital or medical school in your state or your county or city mental health association. (Check the phone book.)

If you are, in fact, suffering from social anxiety disorder or another mental health disorder, such as clinical depression, your treatment plan is likely to include cognitive-behavior therapy and/or a prescription for antidepressant or anti-anxiety drugs. Research shows that the combination of therapy plus medication is the most effective approach to heal many mental health disorders. Cognitive-behavior therapy may involve exposing you to specific situations that frighten you, as well as cognitive restructuring, which teaches you to identify "dangerous" situations and think about them differently so they become less threatening. Group therapy is also a possibility. This form of treatment allows you to practice overcoming your fear of people by meeting weekly with a group. Over time, you learn how to live comfortably in a social environment and eventually generalize this experience to social situations outside of the group. Treatment might also include anxiety management training, which may involve physical relaxation techniques like deep breathing.

Once you receive what you consider to be the right diagnosis for what you've been experiencing, research the latest treatments for that particular disorder. Visit, for example, the Web sites of the American Psychological Association (www.apa.org), the American Psychiatric Association, and the National Institute of Mental Health. You'll get a range of treatment ideas you should be hearing about from the mental health practitioner you've chosen.

Remember, every time you open a new door, you increase your opportunities to more fully experience the gift of life.